D0481346

C.1 0722878

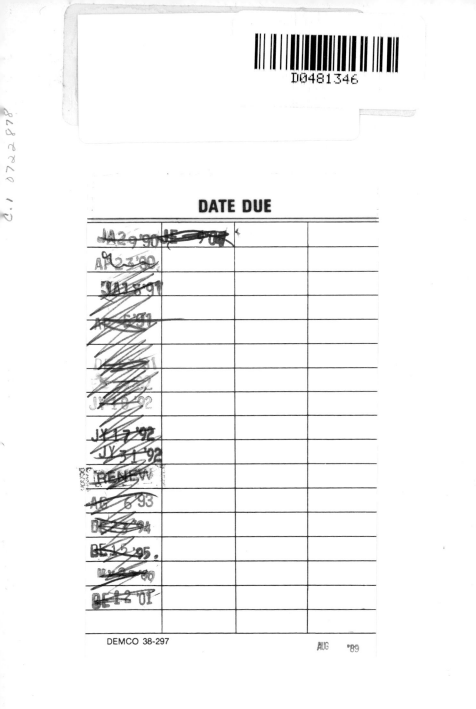

DATE DUE

JA 29 '90			
AP 23 '90			
JA 18 '91			
AP 6 '91			
DE			
JY 10 '92			
JY 17 '92			
JY 31 '92			
RENEW			
AP 6 '93			
DE 27 '94			
DE 15 '95			
NO			
DE 12 '01			

DEMCO 38-297

AUG '89

AMERICA'S ELECTIONS

Opposing Viewpoints®

Other Books of Related Interest in the Opposing Viewpoints Series:

American Government
Civil Liberties
The Mass Media
The Political Spectrum
Social Justice

Additional Books in the Opposing Viewpoints Series:

Abortion
AIDS
American Foreign Policy
The American Military
American Values
America's Prisons
The Arms Race
Biomedical Ethics
Censorship
Central America
Chemical Dependency
Constructing a Life Philosophy
Crime & Criminals
Criminal Justice
Death and Dying
The Death Penalty
Drug Abuse
Economics in America
The Environmental Crisis
Latin America and U.S. Foreign Policy
Male/Female Roles
The Middle East
Nuclear War
Poverty
Problems of Africa
Science and Religion
Sexual Values
The Soviet Union
Teenage Sexuality
Terrorism
The Vietnam War
War and Human Nature

AMERICA'S ELECTIONS

Opposing Viewpoints®

David L. Bender & Bruno Leone, *Series Editors*

Thomas Modl, *Book Editor*

OPPOSING VIEWPOINTS SERIES ®

Greenhaven Press • 577 Shoreview Park Road • St. Paul, Minnesota 55126

Riverside Community College
Library
4800 Magnolia Avenue
Riverside, CA 92506

No part of this book may be reproduced or used in any other form or by any other means, electrical, mechanical or otherwise, including, but not limited to photocopy, recording or any information storage and retrieval system, without prior written permission from the publisher.

Library of Congress Cataloging-in-Publication Data

America's elections : opposing viewpoints / Tom Modl, book editor.
    p.   cm. — (Opposing viewpoints series)
    Bibliography: p.
    Includes index.
    Summary: Presents opposing viewpoints on various aspects of elections in the United States, including who should vote, how elections should be financed, what role political parties should play in elections, and how presidential elections could be reformed.
    ISBN 0-89908-433-8 (lib. bdg.) : $13.95. ISBN 0-89908-408-7 (pbk.) : $6.95
    1. Elections—United States. [1. Elections. 2. Politics, Practical.] I. Modl, Tom, 1963-   . II. Series.
JK1965.A65 1988
324.6973—dc19   87-36788
                                                                CIP
                                                                AC

© Copyright 1988 by Greenhaven Press, Inc.

Every effort has been made to trace owners of copyright material.

"Congress shall make no law . . .
abridging the freedom of speech,
or of the press."

First Amendment to the US Constitution

The basic foundation of our democracy is the first amendment guarantee of freedom of expression. The *Opposing Viewpoints Series* is dedicated to the concept of this basic freedom and the idea that it is more important to practice it than to enshrine it.

Contents

	Page
Why Consider Opposing Viewpoints?	9
Introduction	13

Chapter 1: Are America's Elections Fair?

Chapter Preface	16
1. Voting Promotes Democracy *Mary O'Connell*	17
2. Voting Is Useless *Bob Avakian*	22
3. The Voting Rights Act Protects Minority Votes *Philip P. Frickey*	27
4. The Voting Rights Act Weakens Minority Votes *Peter H. Schuck*	32
5. Bilingual Ballots Should Not Be Used in Elections *Richard K. Kolb*	39
6. Bilingual Ballots Should Be Used in Elections *Robert R. Brischetto*	45
A Critical Thinking Activity: Distinguishing Bias from Reason	49
Periodical Bibliography	51

**Chapter 2: How Should America's Elections
Be Financed?**

Chapter Preface	53
1. Campaign Finance Reform Is Necessary *Elizabeth Drew*	54
2. Campaign Finance Reform Is Not Necessary *Robert J. Samuelson*	59
3. Political Action Committees Are Too Powerful *Fred Wertheimer*	63
4. Political Action Committees Are Not Too Powerful *Phyllis Schlafly*	70
5. Taxpayers Should Finance Political Campaigns *Charles McC. Mathias Jr.*	77
6. Taxpayers Should Not Finance Political Campaigns *Frank J. Fahrenkopf Jr.*	85

A Critical Thinking Activity: Recognizing   89
   Deceptive Arguments
Periodical Bibliography   91

Chapter 3: What Role Should the Media Play in US Elections?

Chapter Preface   93
1. The Media Should Focus on Issues   94
   Keith Blume
2. The Media Should Focus on Who Is Winning   100
   David S. Broder
3. The Media Should Report on Candidates'   107
   Private Lives
   Michael Kinsley
4. The Media Should Not Report on Candidates'   111
   Private Lives
   Ross K. Baker & William Safire
5. Campaign Advertising Is Harmful   117
   Tom Wicker & Pat M. Holt
6. Campaign Advertising Is Not Harmful   121
   Edwin Diamond & Stephen Bates
A Critical Thinking Activity: Distinguishing   125
   Between Fact and Opinion
Periodical Bibliography   127

Chapter 4: How Should US Presidents Be Elected?

Chapter Preface   129
1. The Primary System Should Be Reformed   130
   Charles T. Manatt
2. The Primary System Should Be Weakened   135
   Donald L. Robinson
3. The Primary System Should Remain Unchanged   141
   Michael Nelson
4. The Electoral College Should Be Abolished   149
   Neal R. Peirce & Lawrence D. Longley
5. The Electoral College Should Be Maintained   157
   Nelson W. Polsby & Aaron Wildavsky
A Critical Thinking Activity: Ranking   162
   Concerns in Choosing a President
Periodical Bibliography   164

Appendix of US Political Parties   165
Organizations To Contact   167
Bibliography of Books   169
Index   171

Why Consider Opposing Viewpoints?

"It is better to debate a question without settling it than to settle a question without debating it."

Joseph Joubert (1754-1824)

The Importance of Examining Opposing Viewpoints

The purpose of the Opposing Viewpoints Series, and this book in particular, is to present balanced, and often difficult to find, opposing points of view on complex and sensitive issues.

Probably the best way to become informed is to analyze the positions of those who are regarded as experts and well studied on issues. It is important to consider every variety of opinion in an attempt to determine the truth. Opinions from the mainstream of society should be examined. But also important are opinions that are considered radical, reactionary, or minority as well as those stigmatized by some other uncomplimentary label. An important lesson of history is the eventual acceptance of many unpopular and even despised opinions. The ideas of Socrates, Jesus, and Galileo are good examples of this.

Readers will approach this book with their own opinions on the issues debated within it. However, to have a good grasp of one's own viewpoint, it is necessary to understand the arguments of those with whom one disagrees. It can be said that those who do not completely understand their adversary's point of view do not fully understand their own.

A persuasive case for considering opposing viewpoints has been presented by John Stuart Mill in his work *On Liberty*. When examining controversial issues it may be helpful to reflect on this suggestion:

> The only way in which a human being can make some approach to knowing the whole of a subject, is by hearing what can be said about it by persons of every variety of opinion, and studying all modes in which it can be looked at by every character of mind. No wise man ever acquired his wisdom in any mode but this.

Analyzing Sources of Information

The Opposing Viewpoints Series includes diverse materials taken from magazines, journals, books, and newspapers, as well as statements and position papers from a wide range of individuals, organizations and governments. This broad spectrum of sources helps to develop patterns of thinking which are open to the consideration of a variety of opinions.

Pitfalls To Avoid

A pitfall to avoid in considering opposing points of view is that of regarding one's own opinion as being common sense and the most rational stance and the point of view of others as being only opinion and naturally wrong. It may be that another's opinion is correct and one's own is in error.

Another pitfall to avoid is that of closing one's mind to the opinions of those with whom one disagrees. The best way to approach a dialogue is to make one's primary purpose that of understanding the mind and arguments of the other person and not that of enlightening him or her with one's own solutions. More can be learned by listening than speaking.

It is my hope that after reading this book the reader will have a deeper understanding of the issues debated and will appreciate the complexity of even seemingly simple issues on which good and honest people disagree. This awareness is particularly important in a democratic society such as ours where people enter into public debate to determine the common good. Those with whom one disagrees should not necessarily be regarded as enemies, but perhaps simply as people who suggest different paths to a common goal.

Developing Basic Reading and Thinking Skills

In this book, carefully edited opposing viewpoints are purposely placed back to back to create a running debate; each viewpoint is preceded by a short quotation that best expresses the author's main argument. This format instantly plunges the reader into the midst of a controversial issue and greatly aids that reader in mastering the basic skill of recognizing an author's point of view.

A number of basic skills for critical thinking are practiced in the activities that appear throughout the books in the series. Some of the skills are:

Evaluating Sources of Information   The ability to choose from among alternative sources the most reliable and accurate source in relation to a given subject.

Separating Fact from Opinion   The ability to make the basic distinction between factual statements (those that can be demonstrated or verified empirically) and statements of opinion (those that are beliefs or attitudes that cannot be proved).

Identifying Stereotypes   The ability to identify oversimplified, exaggerated descriptions (favorable or unfavorable) about people and insulting statements about racial, religious or national groups, based upon misinformation or lack of information.

Recognizing Ethnocentrism   The ability to recognize attitudes or opinions that express the view that one's own race, culture, or group is inherently superior, or those attitudes that judge another culture or group in terms of one's own.

It is important to consider opposing viewpoints and equally important to be able to critically analyze those viewpoints. The activities in this book are designed to help the reader master these thinking skills. Statements are taken from the book's viewpoints and the reader is asked to analyze them. This technique aids the reader in developing skills that not only can be applied to the viewpoints in this book, but also to situations where opinionated spokespersons comment on controversial issues. Although the activities are helpful to the solitary reader, they are most useful when the reader can benefit from the interaction of group discussion.

Using this book and others in the series should help readers develop basic reading and thinking skills. These skills should improve the reader's ability to understand what they read. Readers should be better able to separate fact from opinion, substance from rhetoric and become better consumers of information in our media-centered culture.

This volume of the Opposing Viewpoints Series does not advocate a particular point of view. Quite the contrary! The very nature of the book leaves it to the reader to formulate the opinions he or she finds most suitable. My purpose as publisher is to see that this is made possible by offering a wide range of viewpoints which are fairly presented.

David L. Bender
Publisher

Introduction

"The idea that everybody, credentialed or not, gets to participate [in elections] is the most wonderful and audacious thing about democracy."
Robert Kuttner, *The New Republic,* September 7, 1987

Political scientist W. Russell Neumann gives this tongue-in-cheek definition of a voting citizen:

> Whenever possible, the good citizen . . . dutifully reads all the news coverage of the campaign, discusses domestic and international policy issues with friends and colleagues, attentively reads any campaign literature that comes to hand, and participates in nonpartisan forums such as those sponsored by the League of Women Voters or other civic groups. The good citizen might even bring along a pad and several sharpened pencils to take notes.

Most people would agree that such a description is unrealistic. Most citizens decide who to vote for in a much less formal way than the above description suggests. In fact, many do not participate in the election process at all. The US has the lowest voter turnout of any industrialized nation. Some observers believe this is indicative of widespread voter apathy.

Some people, such as radical socialist author Bob Avakian, think this apathy is justified. According to Avakian, elections "are really for the primary purpose of legitimizing the system and the policies of the ruling class, giving them the mantle of a 'popular mandate.'" One person's vote is meaningless, Avakian argues, because elections have become expensive charades. Elections are indeed expensive—in 1986, the average cost of a successful Senate campaign was $3 million. Therefore, critics of the election process contend, an unusually large amount of a candidate's time must be spent obtaining the financial backing to run. Because of this, candidates may have to appease the interests of large donors and political action committees at the expense of the needs and desires of ordinary voters. Critics conclude that the government is for sale and a single vote does not count for much.

Defenders of the American election system argue that voters can make their voices heard if they make the effort to organize. As Mary O'Connell says, "If people really care about an issue or an election, they can work to get others to join them—and together everyone does have a chance of making a difference." They point to the increased opportunities for voters to make decisions during the election process. For example, thirty-seven states currently use primary elections to allow voters to choose which presidential candidate their state delegation will support at the party conventions. Defenders of the electoral system argue that voters who organize for a particular candidate or issue can influence both who a party chooses as its nominee and what constituencies that nominee will be sensitive to if elected. These people believe that through organized effort, individuals have a better chance than ever of influencing an election's outcome. They conclude, therefore, that apathy is not justified.

In *America's Elections: Opposing Viewpoints*, politicians, journalists, and political scientists argue over whether voters can meaningfully influence government actions and policies. The questions debated include: Are America's Elections Fair? How Should America's Elections Be Financed? What Role Should the Media Play in US Elections? and How Should US Presidents Be Elected? The authors' views represent the variety of perceptions Americans have toward the system by which the leaders of their communities, states, and nation are chosen.

Are America's Elections Fair?

Chapter Preface

Is the right to vote sufficient guarantee that citizens will have an impact on the political system? Many civil rights activists argue that for racial and ethnic minorities, voting is not enough: Minorities face election procedures that give unfair advantage to white, English-speaking voters and candidates. But some political observers argue that charges of unfairness are exaggerated. The viewpoints in this chapter debate whether changes are needed in the way elections are run to insure that everyone has a fair chance in the voting process.

> "Not to participate [in elections] seems to me to be at best foolish . . . and at worst morally irresponsible."

Voting Promotes Democracy

Mary O'Connell

In the following viewpoint, Mary O'Connell argues that it is a citizen's moral duty to take part in elections. She contends that claims by nonvoters that the system is corrupt or that their votes don't matter are often merely excuses for being lazy. O'Connell is a free-lance writer and community activist in Chicago.

As you read, consider the following questions:

1. According to the author, what can happen in an election when there is low voter turnout, or when voters are not well informed?
2. According to O'Connell, why is the presence of corrupt politicians not an excuse for avoiding elections?
3. Why does O'Connell find fault with the attitudes some peace and religious activists have toward elective politics?

Mary O'Connell, "The Least You Can Do Is Vote," *U.S. Catholic*, May 1987. Reprinted with the author's permission.

ve just been through a mayoral election here in Chicago. ..een a subject of fierce controversy for months, and a lot of ,ortant decisions were at stake. Yet, despite all the brouhaha, ,nly about 72 percent of the registered voters came out to vote in the primary—meaning that one in four didn't care enough about the city's future to make the short trip to the polling places.

Hundreds of thousands more aren't even registered. That means they can't vote for anyone. They can't help pick a president to handle issues of war and peace or an alderman to worry about garbage, police, property taxes, and other grimy realities of life in a big city.

Voting Counts

Now I'm sure most of these nonregistered, nonvoting people have opinions about these subjects. If you could get them talking at a bar or a backyard barbecue, you'd hear plenty. Still, they don't bother to express their views where they count. They might as well save their breath.

To me, that's Reason Number One for taking politics seriously: because it's where the decisions get made. Not to participate seems to me to be at best foolish (because your claim is not heard) and at worst morally irresponsible (because you're not bothering to translate abstract concerns for "honesty" and "justice" into real human terms). Strong words. But my strong feelings were aroused in part by some people I encountered while doing voter-registration work in Chicago [in 1986].

One building I visited was largely populated with immigrants, judging by the names on the mailboxes. Most residents had trouble understanding English, let alone my spiel about voter registration, so I came up with the bright idea of asking first "Are you a U.S. citizen?"—until I saw the fear on the face of a young woman who quickly slammed the door in my face.

Another building was owned by a prosperous Vietnamese man who told me he *was* a citizen—but looked worried when I told him about voter registration. He wanted to know, if he did register but didn't vote, would the government come and punish him?

A Right To Vote

Reason Number Two to take voting and politics seriously: you have a right to, as a citizen of a democratic country. Millions of other people live in powerlessness and fear, in part because they have no say in public decisions. . . .

If enough people don't participate (and take it seriously), bad things can happen: that's Reason Number Three.

A lot of people who did vote [in 1986] in the primary elections here in Illinois, didn't take the political process seriously. They didn't bother to inform themselves about candidates much below the governor's line. Instead, they contented themselves with voting

18

for good all-American sounding names. They ended up nominating a couple of crackpots from the Lyndon LaRouche army for lieutenant governor and state treasurer. I used to vote like that on the judges' ballot (my system was to vote for all the women, then do "eenie-meenie-minie-mo" with the rest). Then, a few years ago, a friend had a particularly brutal experience in divorce court and ended up losing custody of her daughter. I found the judge's explanation of his actions incomprehensible. Now I check the judicial recommendations of the newspapers and the local bar association; and I don't vote for anyone unless I have some reason to do so.

Ed Gamble. Reprinted with permission.

This all sounds like common sense, right? But a lot of people clearly don't agree with any of this. Their actions (nonregistration and nonvoting) speak pretty loud. But their words can be even louder. I hear arguments like:

"You can't fight City Hall." Sure you can. The question is whether you can *win*. And the answer depends on a whole lot of things: the issue, whose interests are involved, how hard you fight, how many other people you can get involved, how long you stay at it, and how much you learn along the way. Look at government buildings: typically they're massive structures with huge columns, vast domes, echoing rotundas built on a heroic scale to symbolize the authority of government. You can't expect them to fall down

at the first sound of your tin trumpet. But you can expect to find movement and diversity and flexibility and give-and-take inside them even without their having to come tumbling down.

"One vote doesn't make any difference." Right: few elections are decided by one vote. But if people really care about an issue or an election, they can work to get others to join them—and together everyone does have a chance of making a difference. (The more people one gets, the more of a chance.) Besides, genuine political participation is about more than just voting: it demands writing letters, working for candidates, tracking issues, following voting records. It demands finding and using the levers of power. One thoughtful letter to a legislator at least stands a chance of raising some questions: ten or twenty or fifty letters from individual constituents about the same issue force a legislator to pay attention. And, in legislatures, one vote can often decide a hotly fought issue.

Corruption Is No Excuse

"Politicians are all a bunch of crooks." One friend of mine, who worked with me on a public campaign we both cared deeply about, refused to come along when we had an opportunity to present our case to some important officials. His refusal was nonpartisan, he said, and he applied it to all politicians: "I wouldn't go to them," he told me, "if I had AIDS and they had the cure sitting in a little vial on the edge of the desk. Because I know what would happen. They'd say, 'Sure, we'll give it to you, pal; but first, let's make a deal.' And I'd end up having to promise to register the dead voters when I got to the afterlife." Concern about dead people voting may be peculiar to Chicago, where such things have been known to happen; but the general sentiments he expressed are nonetheless widespread.

Sure there are corrupt politicians. And there are also corrupt bankers and businesspeople, doctors and pharmacists, labor leaders and basketball coaches, and maybe even Vatican officials. As an occupation, politics draws its share of knaves and fools but also its geniuses and heroes along with the usual complement of ordinary folk. Decent people who stay out of politics because they believe all politicians are crooks help make their opinion a self-fulfilling prophecy—and they get the kind of government their squeamishness deserves.

Must Work in the System

"Politics is distasteful; absolute issues—like the protection of children, or the abolition of nuclear weapons—get compromised." Politics operates by the same rules that apply wherever people need to cooperate to get things done. (If you doubt that, think about office politics, faculty politics, church politics. They're all piously denied, of course—usually by the people who play them best.) If you want to get something done on this green earth, you have to

cooperate with other people. Admirable goals—like the abolition of weapons—don't happen once and for all. They have to be fought out, in detail, in different seasons and in different places, through public pressure, negotiation, and compromise.

A congressional staffer once vented to me his frustration about people, "especially from religious groups, who come in here with the best-intended statements about feeding starving people and reducing defense expenditures. But they never translate it into the kind of club that you can *use* with a politician, by studying his voting record, challenging his excessive interest in defense contracts, organizing people at the grassroots level in his district. They think that just by making their statement on behalf of peace and justice, everyone will be in awe of their brightness and be redeemed." He went on: "The extent to which you know the issues, really steep yourself in the details, and know how to move the system—that's what creates the possibility of moral action."

Why Should Anyone Vote?

Many people view declining turnout with alarm because of the comparatively low voting rate in the United States and also because winning candidates can, and often do, claim mandates based on the support of only a small minority of the eligible population. . . .

Why should anyone vote? There are four reasons: (1) voting is what democracy is all about; (2) the entire system would collapse if no one voted; (3) voting is the only way that you can be sure that your voice will be heard; and (4) voting is simply important in itself.

Robert E. DiClerico and Eric M. Uslaner, *Few Are Chosen,* 1984.

People who don't want to bother with that kind of effort, who don't even want to bother to register and vote, have that right, of course. But I wish they'd spare me the diatribes against corrupt politicians, or for that matter, the sentimental songs about peace. Because they don't *really* care enough to do anything about it. And that, as I said before, is morally irresponsible.

"Elections . . . and the 'democratic process' as a whole, are a sham."

Voting Is Useless

Bob Avakian

In the following viewpoint, Bob Avakian contends that the electoral process is not truly democratic. Ruling elites in business, politics, and the media instead use elections to legitimize their stranglehold over society. In a system such as this, Avakian contends, those who wish to hold elective office cannot advocate real change, and ordinary voters exert little influence. Avakian is the chairman of the Revolutionary Communist Party, USA.

As you read, consider the following questions:

1. According to the author, how do the media tell people what to think?
2. Why does Avakian believe that no meaningful social change can occur through elections?
3. According to the author, why are the votes of ordinary people unimportant?

Bob Avakian, *Democracy: Can't We Do Better Than That?* Chicago, IL: Banner Press, 1986. Reprinted with permission.

Many will say: how can the political system in a democratic country like the U.S. "serve to maintain the rule of the bourgeoisie over the proletariat" when everyone has the right to choose the political leaders by participating in elections? The answer to this is that elections in such a society, and the "democratic process" as a whole, are a sham—and more than a sham—a cover for and indeed a vehicle through which domination over the exploited and oppressed is carried out by the exploiting, oppressing, ruling class. To state it in a single sentence, elections: are controlled by the bourgeoisie; are not the means through which basic decisions are made in any case; and are really for the primary purpose of legitimizing the system and the policies and actions of the ruling class, giving them the mantle of a "popular mandate," and of channeling, confining, and controlling the political activity of the masses of people.

False Mandates

In relation to all this the [1984] presidential election in the U.S. is highly instructive. The consensus was obviously reached within the ruling class, well before the election, that Reagan was the man for the times; this was transmitted and drummed into people through the media. Again, there was the attempt to disguise it as the popular will (people are told what *to* think by telling them it is what they already *do* think). There was the incessant refrain that Reagan was "unbeatable." All of this to set up an overwhelming "mandate" for what Reagan personifies. And, in any case, should Mondale have somehow won the election, it wouldn't have made the slightest bit of difference on any substantial question—above all on the cardinal question of preparing for war against the rival Soviet bloc.

This is not to say that Reagan has no base of support among people in the U.S. With the intensification of world events—and in particular the all-around crisis of the imperialist system, involving both the Soviet- and U.S.-led blocs, and the heightening rivalry between them, pushing things rapidly toward world war—there is increasing polarization within the U.S. But the basic terms of this polarization are not Republicans versus Democrats (this does involve some real differences, but precisely differences among and on the terms of the ruling class). Rather, the basic polarization is between the ruling class on one side, including both its major parties and all the major political figures paraded before the people, and on the other side the exploited and dispossessed—with a large number of people in between these two basic poles and tending to split and to oscillate between the one and the other. As for elections specifically, to a large degree the proletarians and other oppressed who make up that pole do not vote, or even if they do vote do not put much stock in the notion that this will

Dick Locher. Reprinted by permission: Tribune Media Services.

have any real effect on the decision makers and the direction of things. The molding of public opinion around the elections has its main effect on that "large number of people in between," but it also affects the exploited and dispossessed, particularly by making them feel they are up against a powerful government that has a "popular mandate."

Ruling Class Makes Choices

On the most obvious level, to be a serious candidate for any major office in a country like the U.S. requires millions of dollars—a personal fortune or, more often, the backing of people with that kind of money. Beyond that, to become known and be taken seriously depends on favorable exposure in the mass media (favorable at least in the sense that you are presented as within the framework of responsible—that is, acceptable—politics). These mass media are called that because they reach and influence masses of people daily and constantly. But they are certainly not controlled by the masses, nor do they reflect or serve their fundamental interests. They are themselves key pillars of the power structure: they are owned by major financial interests (where they are not owned by the states) and are in any case closely regulated by the state. By the time "the people express their will through voting," both the candidates they have to choose among and the "issues" that deserve "serious consideration" have been selected out by someone else: the ruling class. Small wonder they are more than willing to abide by the results!

Further, and even more fundamentally, to "get anywhere" once elected—both to advance one's own career and to "get anything done"—it is necessary to fit into the established mold and work within the established stuctures. This is partially because those already entrenched in positions of power and influence are thereby in a position to make others conform and work through the accepted avenues, but more basically it is because, once again, the political system must serve the underlying economic system. This is not a mere theoretical abstraction, it has concrete meaning: policies and actions which work against or undermine that economic system *will in fact* cause disruption, disorder, chaos, breakdowns in the more or less orderly functioning of things— and unless you are prepared to see the entire order overthrown, with all that implies, you can only view such disruption, disorder, and chaos as something to be avoided or kept to the minimum where it cannot be avoided. But if you are prepared to see—and work for—the overthrow of the existing order, and if you say so openly, you will never be allowed to hold any real position of power; or, if, on the other hand, you have this perspective but hide it and attempt to "get in the power structure and work from within," you will be swallowed up—or chewed up and spit out— by that structure. There is an abundance of historical experience to demonstrate this—and none which disproves it.

Votes Don't Mean Anything

If, however, the electoral process in bourgeois society does not represent the exercise of sovereignty by the people, it generally does play an important role in maintaining the sovereignty—the dictatorship—of the bourgeoisie and the continuation of capitalist society. This very electoral process itself tends to cover over the basic class relations—and class antagonisms—in society, and serves to give formal, institutionalized expression to the political participation of atomized individuals in the perpetuation of the status quo. This process not only reduces people to isolated individuals but at the same time reduces them to a passive position politically and defines the essence of politics as such atomized passivity—as each person, individually, in isolation from everyone else, giving his/her approval to this or to that option, *all of which options have been formulated and presented by an active power standing above these atomized masses of "citizens."* It is not infrequently said, as a major selling point of this electoral process (in the USA specifically), that, regardless of everything else—and in particular, regardless of admittedly immense differences in wealth and economic power and social status—the ballot box is the great equalizer . . . that once you step into that polling booth, the vote of a common wage-worker and the vote of a Rockefeller count for the same thing. And, fundamentally, this is true—neither of these votes counts for a damn thing; Rockefeller (or the class of Rockefellers) doesn't need to vote to exercise political power, and the common wage-workers will never exercise political power under this system no matter how many votes they cast or for what. There never has been and never will be "a revolution through the ballot box," not only because the powers-that-be would forcibly suppress any such attempt, but also—and this touches on a very important function of elections in bourgeois society—because the very acceptance of the electoral process as the quintessential political act reinforces acceptance of the established order and works against any radical rupture with, to say nothing of the actual overturning of, that order. In sum, then, the electoral process and the notion that this process represents the expression of the popular will serves not to set or to fundamentally influence the politics that govern society but to reinforce the shackles binding the masses of people to the political—and underlying economic—interests and dictates of the governing, dominant class.

"[The Voting Rights Act] seeks to guarantee that minority groups are not fenced out of the political arena by electoral structures that substantially dilute their vote."

The Voting Rights Act Protects Minority Votes

Philip P. Frickey

The Voting Rights Act was amended in 1982, giving the federal government and the courts power to supervise the drawing of electoral district boundaries. Civil rights advocates had long contended that white politicians dilute minority voting power by spreading minority voters into several districts, or by having at-large elections, where the white majority could elect a slate of candidates to represent the whole community. In the following viewpoint, Philip P. Frickey argues that re-districting under the Voting Rights Act protects minority voters. Frickey is a law professor at the University of Minnesota.

As you read, consider the following questions:

1. Why is the "melting pot" theory of political participation in this country a myth, according to the author?
2. According to Frickey, how does the amended Voting Rights Act give minorities a chance to influence policy in their communities?
3. What are the limits to what the Voting Rights Act can achieve for minorities, according to Frickey?

Philip P. Frickey, "Majority Rule, Minority Rights, and the Right to Vote: Reflections Upon a Reading of Minority Vote Dilution," *Law & Inequality*, July 1985. Reprinted with permission.

The American approach to voting rights has operated on at least two inconsistent levels. One track is based on the simple ideology that the citizenry's right to vote preserves all their other rights. Dr. Martin Luther King, Jr. subscribed to this view, and saw the vote as providing the minority community with the ability to protect itself. It is reported that Chief Justice Warren felt the same: he chose *Baker v. Carr* . . . as his most important constitutional decision "because he believed that if each of us has an equal vote, we are equally armed with the indispensable means to make our views felt."

This philosophy, which permeates the "one person, one vote" concept . . . is linked inexorably to the vision of America as the great melting pot. In this nation of minorities, give all citizens the vote and therefore the same political weapon, so the theory goes, and let them fight out their problems in the pluralistic political arena; the resulting political compromises will not systematically favor any person or group to the exclusion of others, and all citizens will be sufficiently protected in the political struggle. Over time, it is said, the melting-pot phenomenon will homogenize the citizenry, bring minorities into the heart of the American political and economic process, and place sufficient political power in the hands of minorities so that they can fully protect themselves against any residual discrimination. In its most simplistic form, this ideology sees all citizens as fungible once they are free to register and to vote for candidates of their choice.

Ethnic Wards Provide Power

This scenario is a myth, both historically and currently. It is plain beyond doubt that it ignores the warping effect of racial prejudice as well as the legitimate interests of persons of different cultural heritages to develop their own approaches to participating in public life. It does not even accurately reflect its prototypic example, the way in which European immigrants in nineteenth century America supposedly became assimilated in melting-pot fashion. The best structural friend those immigrants had was ward elections—which promote heterogeneity, not homogeneity. When immigrants and their offspring achieved political power in American cities, the white business elite reacted with the "Progressive" notion of at-large electoral schemes, which were adopted at least in part to dilute immigrant political power. It remains true today that, when bloc voting by the white majority is severe and the electoral structure—for example, at-large elections—provides a winner-take-all opportunity to the majority, the minority community is disenfranchised. In this situation, the right to vote does not only fail to preserve all other rights, it is essentially meaningless. Minority citizens perceive this fact, and their disproportionately low voting rate is a rational response to it.

A second, more realistic approach to the right to vote grew out of a recognition of these facts. This approach seeks to guarantee that minority groups are not fenced out of the political arena by electoral structures that substantially dilute their vote. When the courts proved reluctant to embrace this conception of the right to vote, Congress reacted by amending section 2 of the Voting Rights Act. That statute promotes a new vision of the melting-pot theory under which the minority community has a right to be thrown in the pot and, perhaps, retain some of its essential flavor. That approach may seem bold and unwise to judges who persist in the simple melting-pot view and see protections for distinct minority groups as a barrier to social progress.

No Abridgement of Minorities

(a) No voting qualification of prerequisite to voting or standard, practice, or procedure shall be imposed or applied by any State or political subdivision in a manner that results in the denial or abridgement of the right of any citizen of the United States to vote on account of race or color.". . .

(b) A violation of subsection (a) is established if, based on the totality of circumstances, it is shown that the political processes leading to nomination or election in the State or political subdivision are not equally open to participation by members of a class of citizens protected by subsection (a) in that its members have less opportunity than other members of the electorate to participate in the political process and to elect representatives of their choice. The extent to which members of the protected class have been elected to office in the State or political subdivision is one circumstance which may be considered: Provided, [t]hat nothing in this subsection establishes a right to have members of a protected class elected in numbers equal to their proportion in the population.

Voting Rights Act Amendments of 1982, Section 2.

Yet even the new statutory remedy for minority vote dilution envisions the vote as indirectly preservative of other rights. Rather than guaranteeing any policy outcomes favorable to the minority community, amended section 2 simply seeks to provide that community with a fighting chance to win some benefits in the political arena. The new statute continues old traditions by refusing to attack social problems directly and by internalizing social disputes into established political channels. In addition, the statute reflects the same philosophy that led the courts to label certain individual rights of freedom against the state as fundamental while refusing to place affirmative obligations upon the state that would often more dramatically benefit minorities.

Is the fundamental ideology supporting the American approach to voting rights misguided? Minorities have come a long way in American politics. Yet, can we assume that outlawing some demonstrably discriminatory electoral structures will substantially enhance minority political power and result in a more favorable allocation of public resources to the minority community? The alternative, more direct and radical methods of changing existing power relationships in American society, is, it is needless to say, not likely to happen through existing political institutions.

Intervening Locally for Minorities

Yet amended section 2 is not simply another liberal effort to effect incremental social change by tinkering at the margins of our political institutions. To be sure, Congress' overwhelming support for the amendment to section 2 can be simply explained by the power of the ideology supporting voting rights and by the widespread understanding that fair allocation of voting power is a substitute for fundamental social change. It may also reflect that the civil rights community spent much of its limited political influence to achieve the passage of the amendment. If properly interpreted, however, amended section 2, is, by American standards, a surprisingly powerful national intrusion into state and local affairs. To borrow the language of my colleague Gerald Torres from a different context, the statute is not simply a typical liberal effort "to change the complexion of institutions while leaving the structure of those institutions intact." It has the potential to change a number of racially neutral local political structures in the name of racial justice. Even if public policy is not significantly altered by these changes, amended section 2 is a useful precedent for holding the federal government responsible to intervene in intensely local affairs to promote the goals of the fourteenth and fifteenth amendments.

Moreover, amended section 2 somewhat protects minorities against the risks inherent in the present shift from federal to state and local control over public spending. In the 1960s, the federal government pumped billions of dollars into local social programs. Control over those programs rested at the federal level, where minority influence was greater than in many localities. Today, federal money flows to state and local governments with few strings attached, and federal control is minimal. Amended section 2 could provide minorities with greater opportunity to influence how the states and localities use these funds.

As Far as the System Can Go

To be sure, if the goal were to promote social change at more than just an incremental rate, federal intervention should be directed toward the ends of policy, not toward the structure by which policy is made. But identifying and formulating the policy

30

changes necessary to achieve major social change would be intensely controversial, and an overall federal solution could not take account of local concerns. The federal intervention embodied in amended section 2 has a more modest, but still substantial and worthwhile goal. Whether that goal is achieved to any meaningful extent remains to be seen. And, even if structural reform of some local governments does result, we must still question whether it will bring any substantial benefits to the minority community.

An Equitable Number of Minority Districts

During the congressional debate in 1982 opponents of the amendment of Section 2 [of the Voting Rights Act] argued that the results test would have the effect of imposing racial quotas for office holding. To meet these concerns, Congress included a disclaimer in the statute that "nothing in this section establishes a right to have members of a protected class elected in numbers equal to their proportion in the population." Thus, successful plaintiffs in Section 2 cases have no right to such remedies as weighted or cumulative voting, designated minority seats, the use of single transferable ballots or similar procedures which would guarantee minority officeholding. The legislative history does indicate, however, that in reapportionment cases under Section 2, successful plaintiffs are entitled to new plans which create an equitable number of majority black voting districts. Majority black districts do not guarantee proportional representation; they merely insure that minority candidates will not automatically lose solely because of their race.

The American Civil Liberties Union, *The Voting Rights Act*, 1983.

Amended section 2 may represent the practical limit to which federal intervention into state and local affairs is likely to occur in the present American political system. Thus, the answers to these questions will perhaps measure the extent to which minority goals can be achieved in the best of all politically feasible worlds. If this is so, all eyes in the civil rights community—as well as those in other parts of society concerned with racial justice—will focus on the judicial treatment of minority voting rights in the years ahead.

*"From a guarantee of racial minorities' . . .
right to cast ballots, the [Voting Rights] act has
been turned into a kind of racial quota system
for legislators."*

The Voting Rights Act
Weakens Minority Votes

Peter H. Schuck

In the following viewpoint, Peter H. Schuck argues that the Voting
Rights Act no longer just protects the right to vote. Instead, its
proponents and government bureaucrats are using the Act's provisions to set up racially-segregated electoral districts. According
to Schuck, this concentration of minority voters into single-race
districts protects minority officeholders from challenges. It also
allows conservative whites to consolidate their supporters in an
increased number of all-white districts. Schuck believes this
development further isolates minority voters from society as a
whole and weakens their influence. Schuck is a law professor at
Yale University.

As you read, consider the following questions:

1. In what two ways is the Justice Department's enforcement
   of the Voting Rights Act wrong, according to the author?
2. According to the author, why do politicians who have
   traditionally opposed civil rights measures support the
   current interpretation of the Voting Rights Act?

Peter H. Schuck, "What Went Wrong With the Voting Rights Act," *The Washington
Monthly,* November 1987. Reprinted with permission from *The Washington Monthly.*
Copyright by THE WASHINGTON MONTHLY CO., 1711 Connecticut Avenue NW,
Washington, DC 20009. (202) 462-0128.

As every middle-aged reader of the [*Washington*] *Monthly* will recall, the Voting Rights Act of 1965 was swiftly enacted in the wake of the turbulent march on Selma to combat black disenfranchisement in those southern states that had abused literacy tests and other conditions on voting.

The act's success in drawing minorities into electoral activity is unquestionably among the greatest triumphs of modern American politics. Since 1965, black and Hispanic political participation and influence have burgeoned. The number of black elected officials has grown enormously. Black and Hispanic politicians run many of America's largest cities, sit in increasing numbers in Congress and the state legislatures, and occupy influential administrative posts at all levels of government. Hispanics have won gubernatorial races and blacks are poised to do so in some states. Most important, minorities are swing constituencies in many areas still represented by whites; their decisive electoral power has forced segregationist politicians like Strom Thurmond and George Wallace to reverse fervently avowed positions and to court minority political support through patronage, pork, and other concessions. . . .

A Racial Quota

But few may realize that in the years since 1965, the federal courts and the Department of Justice began to implement the act in ways that by 1982 had radically altered its goals and methods. From a guarantee of racial minorities' 15th Amendment right to cast ballots, the act has been turned into a kind of racial quota system for legislators. Federal bureaucrats have invalidated at-large electoral systems, packing minorities into single member disticts so that only members of their group can win.

Congress has approved these changes and steadily enlarged the act's scope. Most recently, in 1982, it made voting rights violations easier to prove and extended the act's "emergency" provisions, originally slated to expire in 1970, until the year 2007. Although these amendments specified that they were not intended to create proportional representation by race, they have been used to advance that very purpose. Instead of insuring equal political opportunities for minorities, the act is now interpreted to prescribe electoral outcomes, enforced by racial allocations of legislative seats.

This evolution of the Voting Rights Act, Abigail Thernstrom writes . . . is "controversial policy that has somehow stirred no controversy." The long awaited appearance of her book [*Whose Votes Count?*] will change all that.

The Voting Rights Act was a striking political innovation with immediate, far-reaching effects. Its central provision prohibited any qualification that limited voting rights. But it also adopted three "emergency" provisions that would expire, unless renewed, in five years. One prohibited literacy tests or similar devices in those jurisdictions where they had been used and where voter registration or turnout in the 1964 presidential election was below 50 percent—southern states. Another authorized the appointment of federal voting examiners in those jurisdictions. The third required local and state governments to obtain Department of Justice "preclearance" of almost all changes in voting rules and procedures.

Thernstrom's story, written with scrupulous balance and obvious sympathy for the cause of racial justice, reveals numerous ironies. The South's long political oppression of blacks ended up empowering them. States' Rights claims triggered a far more intrusive federal intervention than anything since Reconstruction. The Nixon administration's "southern strategy" to lure southern Democratic voters into the GOP played directly into the hands of the civil rights groups; in order to destigmatize a law that was decidedly regional at inception, the act was extended in 1970 to the entire nation.

Leaving Minorities Isolated

The pressure for . . . interracial, interethnic coalitions lessens with the existence of single-member districts drawn to maximize minority officeholding. Political necessity brings groups together. The majority-white county, city, or district in which whites vote as a solid bloc against any minority candidate is now unusual. Especially in districts or localities with a substantial minority population, divisions among white voters send white candidates scurrying for those important black votes. The process not only enhances political integration but also may serve to heighten minority electoral influence. . . .

Candidates who have joined hands in a victorious biracial coalition will tend to stick together on a governing body, since the next election is never far off. But when whites on a city council or other legislative body owe nothing to black support, blacks in the minority may find themselves consistently outvoted and thus isolated.

Abigail Thernstrom, *Whose Votes Count?*, 1987.

"The more potent the legislation became," Thernstrom observes, "the fewer were the objections raised. As the scope of the act was enlarged, the ranks of its opponents thinned." Congressional hearings in 1975 which turned up little evidence of Hispanic disenfranchisement, were used to expand the act to cover Hispanics and other language minorities. In 1982, the most conservative administration in a half century, allied with a Republican-controlled Senate and a reactionary Judiciary Committee chairman, Strom

Thurmond, stood by while Congress adopted amendments that contradicted every ideological principle this alliance stood for. And the administration's civil rights chief, William Bradford Reynolds, vilified by minority group spokesmen for his passionate opposition to extensive affirmative action, implemented the act in ways that reinforced that very remedy and strengthened his critics.

Bureaucrats Shaping Elections

The most important irony, though, was the transformation of the preclearance provision. Originally, preclearance was intended as a temporary adjunct to the ban on literacy tests and similar devices, enabling the Department of Justice (or the federal court in Washington) to insure that southern states covered by the act could not use new subterfuges to circumvent that ban. Under Republican and Democratic administrations alike, preclearance became the act's central regulatory mechanism. Prodded by civil rights groups and incumbent politicians, the Justice Department extended the provision's scope far beyond voting and registration procedures. Municipal annexations, court-ordered redistrictings, multimember districting, at-large voting or majority vote rather than plurality requirements in elections, and other decisions by elected officials cannot go into effect until they are approved by staff attorneys in the Voting Rights Section of Justice's Civil Rights Division. In this way, bureaucratic lawyers are reshaping politics from Opelika, Alabama to New York City.

Thernstrom reveals, with devastating effect, what happened when vast regulatory power was placed at the service of a great but ill-defined ideal. It is not a pretty picture. The department lawyers, she argues, wore ideological blinders. Using high-minded euphemisms to cover their tracks, they defined political equality as requiring "safe legislative seats corresponding to a minority's share of the population." To compensate for low minority turnout and registration, the department has defined a "safe seat as one with 65 percent minority voters and with no strong white candidate." To secure these seats against competition from white candidates, the department has decided that at-large and multimember districting systems must go the way of hoop skirts.

The department's position, Thernstrom maintains, is wrong on two counts. First, it is contrary to the law; the Supreme Court has consistently held that proportional representation is neither the constitutional nor the statutory standard that electoral systems must meet. Second, it is a highly dubious policy. While creating safe seats increases the number of minority office holders, it dissipates minority voters' influence over the process as a whole. Packing minority voters into a few districts that they can safely control relinquishes almost all minority influence in the far larger number of districts now populated almost entirely by whites. Conservative politicians, lacking the moderating influence of a black constituency, feel freer to move toward the political extreme. Single-member districting can breed corrupt, parochial, machine politics as in Chicago and other cities. At the turn of the century, Progressive reformers adopted at-large and multimember systems to force candidates to reach out across ethnic and neighborhood lines, thereby encouraging more public-spirited, integrated politics. Nevertheless, Thernstrom observes, "no amount of argument can persuade the Justice Department that it is legitimate to divide black voters between districts in order to protect a white liberal incumbent who has served that black community well, and who perhaps has seniority on legislative committees that are important to blacks."

A Strange and Sad Call

Creating black districts is a limited answer, best resorted to in only the worst cases. One-third of all black mayors, after all, are elected from white majority towns. It is a mistake to assume that all of America is Mississippi in 1957, that whites cannot be made responsive to blacks, and that it is better to go it alone than build bridges. That is a strange and sad call from those who rightly promote integration in other aspects of our daily lives.

Matthew Cooper, *The Washington Monthly*, February 1987.

In its 1980 *Bolden* decision, the Supreme Court ruled that constitutional challenges to an electoral system (as distinguished from challenges under the Voting Rights Act) could succeed only upon proof that these systems were adopted or implemented with discriminatory *intent*. Minority challengers thus bore a difficult burden of proof. Many electoral systems had been adopted decades earlier and evidence of the legislators' original purpose was nearly impossible to assemble.

When the Voting Rights Act came up for renewal in 1982, civil rights groups, skillfully mobilized by the Leadership Conference on Civil Rights, argued that the crucial question was not intent but whether the electoral structure resulted in the dilution of minority votes. Earlier court decisions had based findings of vote dilution upon a combination of factors other than intent, including a history of racial-bloc voting, unresponsiveness to minority concerns, at-large or multimember districting systems, and failure to elect minority group candidates. Relying upon these precedents, the Leadership Conference pressed for an amendment to permit minorities to prevail if they could prove discriminatory *results*.

The Leadership Conference sought to convince Congress that its proposed amendment merely restored the pre-*Bolden* standard for constitutional violations and extended it to statutory voting discrimination claims. The difficulty with a results test is the amount of discretion that it confers on the courts and its potential, especially when administered by judges with limited leverage over a complex political process, to degenerate into a race-based numbers game and ultimately into racially proportional representation.

Although there were other remedies for that danger, such as making clear the types of circumstantial evidence that would prove discriminatory intent, the Leadership Conference pressed for an unqualified results test. Its tactic succeeded in the House, where civil rights workhorse, Rep. Don Edwards, conducted low-visibility hearings. The fireworks in the Republican-controlled Senate, however, left no doubt that courts might use the new "results" language to strike down *all* electoral systems that impeded proportional representation. . . .

Thernstrom contends that these interpretations are propelling us down a slippery slope to a politics of explicit race-based entitlements akin to India's caste system. She may well be right. Earlier this year, the Justice Department issued new guidelines that reinforce its gerrymandering strategy. . . . The Supreme Court agreed to hear challenges to *party*-based gerrymandering, which can be adjudicated only by applying a proportional representation standard. Manhattan Republicans, it appears, can now go to court to complain of voting rights discrimination.

Real Racial Justice

To Thernstrom, the courts and the Justice Department have quietly perverted Congress's intent and have abused the judicial and administrative processes. Her account, however, justifies a rather different and in some ways more interesting and disturbing conclusion. Congress amended and extended the act in 1982 with its eyes wide open. Insofar as members ever understand the complex questions on which they vote, they knew—especially in the Senate, where the issue was clearly drawn—that the department and the courts were using the act to move towards racially proportional representation. Bland euphemisms and high-minded rhetoric may have made it easier for politicians to ignore the reality, but in the end they blessed and even accelerated the law's transformation.

Suppose the original Voting Rights Act had instead been entitled the "Racial Gerrymandering Act," elaborated in the statute's preamble as "An act to authorize bureaucrats and judges to guarantee safe seats to minority candidates." Is it conceivable that Congress would have enacted it or that the Supreme Court would have upheld its constitutionality? To pose the question, of course, is to answer it. . . .

Packing minority voters into a few districts is good politics not just for minority candidates but for Republicans and conservative Democrats as well. Draining blacks from white districts, as Thernstrom shows, weakens liberals and moderate candidates and strengthens their opponents on the right. This disadvantage might be outweighed if minority constituents packed into a few districts, represented by persons of their own race, reaped more benefits than if their influence was exerted on a larger number of representatives, black or white. But no one has demonstrated this to be true, and there are reasons to doubt it.

A Communal, Integrated Politics

The act's original purposes—to protect minority voters against discriminatory voting tests and to equalize electoral opportunity— were quickly achieved. Even when contrived by federal gerrymanders, the election of minority candidates has probably raised many minority voters' political consciousnesses and carries a symbolic importance essential to democratic politics.

But in the long run, the interests of minority voters, as distinct from those of minority candidates, are probably better served by a different strategy that would return to the act's original vision of equal political opportunity. While thwarting all majority efforts to weaken minority gains, it would reject the kind of "benign" racialism that we increasingly take for granted. Instead, it would encourage a more communal, integrative politics in which the politicians (usually white) who control the larger process must, in their own self-interest, compete for minority votes by taking minority demands seriously. In the end, that form of politics, not a paternalistic policy of electoral apartheid, will be the firmest foundation for enduring racial justice.

"Knowledge of English is a rudimentary requirement of U.S. citizenship."

Bilingual Ballots Should Not Be Used in Elections

Richard K. Kolb

One of the provisions of the 1975 revision of the Voting Rights Act authorized the use of bilingual ballots to aid citizens whose primary language was not English. Critics of this provision argue that printing ballots with more than one language will lead to factionalism in American society. In the following viewpoint, Richard K. Kolb contends that the English language is what holds the ethnically diverse United States together. According to Kolb, bilingual ballots undermine this unity, and are part of an effort by some ethnic groups to set themselves apart from the rest of society. Kolb is a member of U.S. English, an organization working to make English the official language of the United States.

As you read, consider the following questions:

1. Why does the author think that the bilingual ballot provision of the Voting Rights Act is unnecessary? What examples does he give to support his argument?
2. What is Kolb's response to the argument that Spanish is as much an American language as English is, and therefore should be on the ballot?
3. According to the author, what is the danger in allowing more than one language to be used in elections and government?

Richard K. Kolb, "Bilingual Ballots: Balkanization of the U.S.," *Human Events,* August 18, 1984. Reprinted with permission.

Bilingualism is a byproduct of the '60s civil rights crusades and '70s "ethnic chic." Abigail Thernstrom noted that it can be traced to a "... profound alienation from American values and commitment to cultural pluralism [that] had moved from the political left to the liberal center."

Bilingual Ballots

Amendments to the Voting Rights Act require local election officials to provide foreign language ballots and voting materials in places where (1) More than 5 per cent of the citizens of voting age are of a single language minority who do not speak English adequately enough to participate in the electoral process; and (2) the illiteracy rate of such persons as a group is higher than the national average (measured by the rate of completion of the fifth grade). The law affects 376 jurisdictions in 19 states.

Congress arbitrarily designated American aborigines, Asians and those of "Spanish heritage" worthy of special treatment. At the time, eight million people spoke foreign tongues in their households; by 1980 the figure had ballooned to 22 million or 11 per cent of the population.

Opposition to the 1975 amendment was muted—it was scarcely debated. Only 70 congressmen and 12 senators voted against multilingual ballots. President Ford eagerly approved the measure with an election year nearing. Attempts to strike the special language provision failed in the House (284-128) in October 1981 and the Senate (54-32) in June 1982. Due to expire in 1985, the provision's life was extended to Aug. 6, 1992.

An Absurd Idea

Practical applications of the law abound in absurdity. Some Alaskan natives, for example, do not have a written language, so voting instructions must be given orally. San Francisco was ordered not merely to provide foreign language ballots, but to actively seek people to utilize them.

Hawaii expended $50,000 to implement the program in 1976 and only 191 persons used the special ballots. Residents there sued to be excluded from the law in 1978. Morris Takushi, then election administrator, said of immigrants: "They came to America by choice and are proud of their new country and new identity as Americans."

California, hardest hit by the amendment, spent $1,282,984 on multilingual materials in 1982. Kings County spent $3,600 per ballot—a grand total of eight voters in the primary and general elections used non-English ballots. Last year, another county shelled out $6,619 and no one utilized them.

Ethnic activists are fond of justifying bilingualism with the specious "historic language" argument. According to Raul Yzaguirre, president of the National Council of La Raza (The Race), an Hispanic advocacy group founded in 1968, "We were here for hundreds of years before the Pilgrims but were conquered and became a colonized people."

Since this contention is central to demands for bilingualism, it is worth in-depth historical examination. The United States commemorated its 400th anniversary on July 13, 1984. On that date in 1584 the English began the colonization of North America at Roanoke Island. "Had it been otherwise," says historian David Stick, "those of us living here today might well be speaking Spanish instead of English."

The Case Against Bilingual Ballots

Opponents of federally mandated voting in foreign languages want [it] repealed. The case for repeal is based on the following considerations:

• English ballots do not prohibit anyone from voting. Anyone who needs help can bring an interpreter into the voting booth.

• Bilingual ballots are deeply resented by millions of earlier immigrants who had to learn English in order to participate in the political process.

• Bilingual ballots are highly symbolic of the official recognition won by other languages, in competition with English.

• Bilingual ballots dissolve the traditional bond between English and citizenship.

• Bilingual ballots are unnecessary, as virtually all applicants for U.S. citizenship must pass an examination demonstrating knowledge of simple English.

• Bilingual ballots invite abuse. A check of San Francisco bilingual ballot users in 1981 disclosed that 20% were not U.S. citizens.

• Bilingual ballots are discriminatory. Only selected languages are targeted for special treatment under the law.

• Bilingual ballots are costly. While the cost of English ballots is usually less than $2.00 per registered voter, non-English ballots range from $6.00 upward. The cost of foreign language ballots to California taxpayers, for instance, is $1.3 million annually.

U.S. English, fact sheet, "Bilingual Voting Ballots," April 1987.

Though Spanish St. Augustine preceded Jamestown by 42 years, only a few thousand Spaniards had settled in Florida by the time it was annexed in 1821. Spaniards occupied what is now New Mexico in 1598 but were driven out in 1680 by Pueblo Indians. The region was reconquered during the next decade. However, a mere 25,000 Spaniards lived there when the Mexican War ended in 1848.

Today, there are about 850,000 descendants of the original *Hispano* settlers spread throughout the Southwest. Other Mexican Cession territories were likewise sparsely populated: the 5,000

Spaniards in California were soon totally absorbed.

Texas entered the Union with only 6,000 Spanish-speakers. Twice as many Germans—13,000—lived in the Lone Star State in 1845. The vast majority of Mexicans crossed the Rio Grande after the Mexican Revolution erupted in 1910. Amerindians are the only group that have a valid claim to historic language rights in the Southwest.

Some 15,000 French settlers inhabited Louisiana at the time of the purchase in 1803. Residents readily accepted English as the official language as a condition of statehood in 1812. In modern times, Acadian cultural aspirations have never engendered national political demands.

German has been thrown up *ad nauseam* as an historical example of American bilingualism. German never received any national official recognition. To assert that because my surname is German (Germans settled in Pennsylvania 300 years ago), this entitles that language to equal status with English is ludicrous.

Other Bilingual Nations

A look at the course of language conflicts in other Western nations is most enlightening. Linguistic militancy and violence toppled the Belgian government in 1968. Constitutionally mandated "linguistic frontiers" and "zones" separate Dutch-speaking Flemings from French-speaking Walloons. Relations, nevertheless, still remain hostile between the segregated "communities.". . .

Canada—"two nations warring in the bosom of a single state"— has been officially bilingual since 1969. In excess of $4 billion has gone toward implementing the law. Some 75 per cent of Canadians speak English.

Quebec demanded and received bilingualism nationally while institutionalizing discrimination within its own province. Since 1977, English has become "permissible between consulting adults and then only in private," said one businessman.

A Commission for the Surveillance of the French Language enforces French-only statutes with a vengeance. Dr. Laurin, the province's cultural ayatollah, dismisses Canada as an entity "which sometimes claims to be a 'nation.'"

The separatist Quebec party calls for a "sovereignty association" or an independent nation within a Canadian economic union. Polls indicate that about 40 per cent of Quebec's population favors this course.

Establishment WASPs, in an effort to atone for alleged past sins, have overseen the transformation of Canada not into a unified nation of citizens with a common identity but one divided into bureaucratic entities bizarrely labeled "francophones" and "anglophones.". . .

Few countries in the world even tolerate [much less]. . .promote the fragmentation of their own national culture. Bilingual programs for immigrants are nonexistent in Latin America. As a longtime resident of Mexico observed, "They want their own culture and language to prevail."

If the advocates of "multi-lingualism" have their way, America, too, will soon be faced with the prospect of "linguistic frontiers," "cantonization," "devolution," "sovereignty association" or some other thinly veiled form of language separatism.

Bilingualism in this country is virtually a code-word for Spanish. Hispanics (an umbrella term for all Spanish-speakers, of whom 60 per cent trace their origins to Mexico) constitute 6.4 per cent of the U.S. population. The vast majority of Hispanics have at least a working knowledge of English if not complete fluency. . . .

Hispanics constitute an important swing bloc in the Southwest and some large urban areas.

This is precisely why politicos will not oppose bilingual ballots. The 1975 amendment, in effect, was a transparent scheme to make political capital by promoting our differences. As former Sen. S.I. Hayakawa said, "Some politicians will do anything that a minority group asks of them, even at the cost of injustice to the majority."

Cries for "Brown Power" have faded since the passage of the amendment. Instead, militants now lead voter-registration drives. No longer is the La Raza Unida party necessary. The Democratic party serves as the vehicle for Chicano political aspirations. . . .

The Language of the Voting Booth

S.I. Hayakawa, former U.S. Senator and Honorary Chairman of U.S. English, commented that "the message is clear, and will reverberate across America: the language we share is at the core of our identity as citizens, and our ticket to full participation in American political life. We can speak any language we want at the dinner table, but *English* is the language of public discourse, of the marketplace, and of the voting booth."

U.S. English, fact sheet, "Bilingual Voting Ballots," April 1987.

As far back as 1820, future Congressman Edward Everett warned, "From the days of the Tower of Babel, confusion of tongues has ever been one of the most active causes of political misunderstanding."

More recently, Sen. Alan Simpson (R.-Wyo.) reminded us that "If linguistic and cultural separatism rise above a certain level, the unity and political stability of the nation will in time be seriously eroded."

America has reached that level. Society is replete with disincentives—foreign TV programs, road signs, drivers' license tests, civil service exams, lottery tickets, multilingual education and voting materials—to learn English.

The English language is society's adhesive just as Anglo-Saxon institutions cement our civic foundations. Government has an obligation to serve as custodian of the core values and preserve the nation's heritage. Hayakawa's 1981 amendment and his subsequent "sense of the Senate" resolution sought to enshrine the primacy of English.

To this end, the former senator and like-minded citizens initiated a grassroots movement in January 1983. "U.S. English" has since grown to a body of 55,000 concerned Americans. Goals include passage of the English Language Amendment, repeal of the 1975 multilingual ballot provision, reform of bilingual education programs and control of immigration that reinforces language separatism. . . .

Cultural Death Wish

Flirtation with multilingualism is a cultural "death wish." Ralph Waldo Emerson wrote: "We infer the spirit of the nation in great measure from the language, which is a sort of monument to which each forcible individual in a course of many hundreds of years has contributed a stone." Those foundation stones are beginning to crumble.

Miami's Mayor Maurice Ferre was absolutely correct when he said, "The thing that rescues people is pride—pride in their religion, their family, their tradition, their language." The great English writer Samuel Johnson (1709-1784) put it even more succinctly: "Languages are the pedigrees of nations." And the pedigree of America is the English language. It will remain so if we wish to survive as a united nation.

Immigrants in America have always been free to retain pride in their origins, but they have also entered into an unwritten compact by making this nation their new home. Knowledge of English is a rudimentary requirement of U.S. citizenship.

Perhaps President Theodore Roosevelt put it best:

"We have room for but one language here, and that is the English language, for we intend to see that the crucible turns out people as Americans, of American nationality, and not as dwellers in a polyglot boardinghouse."

"The presence of Spanish language assistance in the electoral process . . . [is] a sign that Mexican Americans in general are welcomed and encouraged to participate."

Bilingual Ballots Should Be Used in Elections

Robert R. Brischetto

Proponents of bilingual ballots argue that there are many American citizens, particularly in the southwestern United States, who do not speak or read English well enough to take part in elections conducted only in English. In the following viewpoint, Robert R. Brischetto contends that a significant minority of Mexican American citizens can only understand Spanish. He also argues that bilingual ballots make minorities more inclined to take part in the electoral process, regardless of their proficiency at English. Brischetto works with the Southwest Voter Registration Education Project, an organization working to increase Hispanic American participation in elections.

As you read, consider the following questions:

1. Why does Brischetto believe that bilingual ballots will not be as necessary in the future as they are now?
2. What are the different degrees of language ability found among Mexican Americans, according to the author?
3. In the author's opinion, what social groups among Mexican Americans are most likely to need bilingual ballots to be able to vote?

Robert R. Brischetto, *Bilingual Elections at Work in the Southwest: Executive Summary.* Los Angeles, CA: Mexican American Legal Defense and Education Fund, 1982. Reprinted with permission.

A paucity of information on the impact of bilingual elections and their need and usage prompted the Mexican American Legal Defense and Educational Fund (MALDEF) to undertake this study. *Bilingual Elections at Work in the Southwest* presents the results of our research. The findings indicate that the bilingual elections provisions of the Voting Rights Act have had a positive effect on Mexican American participation in the political process. Surveys of 912 U.S. citizens of Mexican descent in three communities [San Antonio, East Los Angeles, and Uvalde County, Texas] reveal that:

• One in seven citizens of Mexican descent do not speak English.

• Bilingual ballots and oral assistance were generally available in the three communities during the 1980 election. However, little outreach effort was made by the counties to provide bilingual materials and assistance in registration.

• One in four Mexican American voters used bilingual ballots in the 1980 Presidential election and as many received bilingual oral assistance when it was made available.

• The availability of bilingual assistance has a symbolic as well as a practical significance for Mexican Americans: almost one-third of all respondents, including some who speak English, said they would be less likely to register and vote if Spanish language assistance were not available. . . .

Many Citizens Speak Spanish

Two national surveys provide data that indicate a number of patterns with regard to Spanish language maintenance for this report. The Census Bureau's Survey of Income and Education (SIE) reports that Spanish speakers comprise two out of every five non-English speakers in the United States (even though only one out of every sixteen persons in the total population are Hispanic). From the National Chicano Survey and the SIE, it is clear that:

1) The vast experience of most Hispanics was that of growing up in a Spanish-speaking household. Only one in seven grew up in English-speaking households.

2) A sizeable number of persons of Mexican origin (16.7% or 830,000) still speak only Spanish. This is true even for native Hispanics.

3) Bilingualism is the predominant pattern of language usage; however, it is important to distinguish between bilinguals as predominantly English or Spanish-speaking.

4) The persistence of Spanish usage has a close association with English language ability. Segments of the Hispanic population exhibit some difficulty in speaking and understanding English. These difficulties are more pronounced for reading and writing skills.

5) A sizeable segment of the Hispanic population functions more frequently and effectively in Spanish than in English.

The MALDEF and Southwest Voter Registration Education Project (SVREP) surveys in three communities confirm the general patterns found in the national samples and demonstrate even greater need for bilingual election services. One in seven citizens surveyed report they speak only Spanish; in addition, four out of five are bilingual. Two-thirds of the bilingual citizens grew up in households where Spanish was the only language spoken, and one in three feel more comfortable speaking Spanish than English. Spanish monolingualism is admittedly diminishing from one generation to the next; while one out of three elderly citizens (age 65 or more) speak only Spanish, one in twenty young Chicano citizens are Spanish monolinguals. This would seem to indicate that the need for bilingual election services will diminish in time. . . .

Bilingual Ballots Promote Assimilation

In the mid-'70s the Voting Rights Act was extended into the Southwest and bilingual ballots were included in the provisions of the original Act. Prior to the extension of this Act in the Southwest, Hispanics had some 1,500 elected officials, according to Harry Pachon, executive director of the National Association of Latin Elected and Appointed Officials (NALEO). In a little over 10 years since this Act was passed, there has been a 100 percent increase in Hispanic elected officials. If the sponsors of English Only simply want language minorities to succeed in assimilating, why do they want to destroy a bill that has brought record numbers of Hispanics into the fold?

Richard T. Castro, *In These Times*, February 18/24, 1987.

A substantial segment of the Mexican American voters in the three communities surveyed were found to have used bilingual materials or assistance when they voted in 1980. On the average, one in four voters reported receiving oral assistance from a bilingual poll worker, when such assistance was available. One in four Hispanic voters reported using some or all of the Spanish translation on the ballot where it was available, ranging from one in ten in East Los Angeles to one-third in Uvalde County. Those most likely to use the Spanish portion of the ballot and to receive assistance from bilingual poll workers were Spanish monolinguals, persons over age 65, persons who were very low in educational attainment (less than five years) and low-income persons. It is clear that the Spanish language assistance and materials are being used to a significant degree, especially by those marginal groups that have demonstrated a need for these services.

Respondents in the three communities surveyed were asked their opinions of bilingual election services and what effect discontinuance of bilingual services would likely have on their participation in the electoral process. One out of three Hispanic citizens indicated they would be less likely to vote without Spanish oral assistance and without a bilingual ballot. As many as seven out of ten Spanish monolingual voters, more than half of all voters with less than five years of schooling and almost half of voters with less than $5,000 annual income said they would be less likely to vote if bilingual election services were eliminated.

Mexican Americans Feel Welcome

The survey results indicate a general perception of the importance of Spanish language assistance in the electoral process. Fully 95 percent of the citizens in the sample indicated it was a good idea to provide language assistance in registration and voting, and 94 percent were convinced it was a good idea to provide a bilingual ballot.

The responses to these opinion questions indicate there is even greater support for bilingual services than actual use of them. These findings suggest that there is a significant symbolic aspect to Spanish language assistance for Mexican American voters apart from the functional linguistic need for these services. The presence of Spanish language assistance in the electoral process may be taken as a sign that Mexican Americans in general are welcomed and encouraged to participate regardless of which language they use. . . .

Conclusion

Surveys in three communities with large concentrations of Mexican American voters indicate that bilingual election materials and services are generally made available, but that outreach efforts are wanting, particularly in regard to bilingual voter registration. Field interviews with election officials and minority community leaders in two of these counties revealed the haphazard manner in which bilingual registration and election services have been administered in these communities.

In spite of these shortcomings, the study shows minority language election services are essential to participation by certain subgroups of minority voters—the elderly, the undereducated, the poor, and Spanish monolinguals. Beyond that, bilingual elections seem to have symbolic value for most citizens of Mexican origin. In their own estimation, removal of these services would have a detrimental effect on their future electoral participation.

Distinguishing Bias from Reason

When dealing with controversial issues, many people allow their feelings to dominate their powers of reason. Thus, one of the most important critical thinking skills is the ability to distinguish between statements based upon emotion or bias and conclusions based upon a rational consideration of the facts.

The following statements are taken from the viewpoints in this chapter. Consider each statement carefully. *Mark R for any statement you believe is based on reason or a rational consideration of the facts. Mark B for any statement you believe is based on bias, prejudice, or emotion. Mark I for any statement you think is impossible to judge.*

If you are doing this activity as a member of a class or group, compare your answers with those of other class or group members. Be able to defend your answers. You may discover that others come to different conclusions than you do. Listening to the rationale others present for their answers may give you valuable insights in distinguishing between bias and reason.

> R = *a statement based upon reason*
> B = *a statement based upon bias*
> I = *a statement impossible to judge*

1. If all the decent people stayed out of politics because they thought all politicians were crooks, they would create a self-fulfilling prophecy.

2. To "get anywhere" once elected it is necessary to fit into the established mold.

3. The need for bilingual ballots will diminish in time, as with each generation there are fewer Hispanic Americans who speak only Spanish.

4. Congress arbitrarily designated American aborigines, Asians and those of "Spanish heritage" worthy of special treatment.

5. "Progressive" notions of election reform, such as at-large elections, were adopted to dilute immigrant and minority power.

6. By requiring federal approval of election system changes, the Voting Rights Act gives minorities a chance to overcome a local majority's efforts to keep minorities out of office.

7. The Voting Rights Act is being used to allocate legislative seats by race.

8. Some activists think that by just making their statement for peace and justice, everyone will be in awe of their brightness and be redeemed.

9. The vote of the wage earner and the vote of the Rockefeller count for just as much—neither is worth a damn thing.

10. Since most Hispanics are less likely to vote if bilingual ballots are not available, bilingual ballots are essential if Hispanic Americans are to participate in the political process.

11. Those who tolerate bilingual ballots are undermining the unity of the American nation.

12. When a white majority consistantly votes for white candidates only, and elections are held at large, minority candidates have little chance of winning.

13. Racially integrated politics, not electoral apartheid, will be the firmest foundation for racial justice.

Periodical Bibliography

The following articles have been selected to supplement the diverse views presented in this chapter.

Walter Dean Burnham	"Elections as Democratic Institutions," *Society,* May/June 1987.
Nicholas von Hoffman	"Death of the Party," *The New Republic,* April 14, 1986.
Rick Jahnkow	"The Ballot Trap," *The Progressive,* August 1987.
Andrew Kopkind	"The 'New Voters' Find Their Voice," *The Nation,* November 7, 1987.
Robert Kuttner	"Why Americans Don't Vote," *The New Republic,* September 7, 1987.
Manning Marable	"Black Politics in Crisis," *The Progressive,* January 1987.
Dick Meister	"Remember, We've Got the Secret Ballot," *The Christian Science Monitor,* October 28, 1986.
Ralph Nader	"Why Voter Turnout Is Turning Off," *The New York Times,* November 4, 1986.
The New Republic	"Democracy's Rusty Weapon," April 14, 1986.
Daniel Pedersen	"All These Guys Owe Willie: An Activist Builds Hispanic Clout at the Grass Roots," *Newsweek,* March 16, 1987.
Kay L. Schlozman and Sidney Verba	"Sending Messages, Getting Replies," *Society,* May/June 1987.
Abigail Thernstrom	"'Voting Rights' Trap: The Danger of Resegregation," *The New Republic,* September 2, 1985.
USA Today	"Politics: What Makes Voters Tick?" April 1986.
Raymond E. Wolfinger	"Registration Creates an Obstacle," *The New York Times,* November 4, 1986.

How Should America's Elections Be Financed?

Chapter Preface

The debate over campaign finance focuses on whether campaign contributions are a way to buy influence or are a form of political expression.

Those who believe private campaign contributions are a way for certain voters to influence the policies of elected officials argue that such contributions harm the political process. These critics contend that once in office, candidates may make policy decisions in favor of their contributors' interests in order to preserve their funding for the next election. These elected officials then may become more concerned about funding their re-election campaigns than they are about the effect their policies will have on their constituents or on the nation.

To defenders of private contributions, however, the act of writing out a check for a candidate is an expression of democracy. They argue that people have the right to spend as much as they want in order to promote their causes and beliefs. They further argue that such spending does not overly influence elected officials. There are so many diverse interests competing for influence that an official can strike a compromise between the conflicting demands and thus avoid being controlled by any single contributor. Private contributions, these defenders contend, are simply an extension of the democratic process and reflect the diversity of the voters.

The viewpoints in this chapter debate whether campaign contributions are becoming an ever-more brazen form of buying influence or are a way in which citizens can express their wishes through the domocratic process.

"Until the problem of money is dealt with, it is unrealistic to expect the political process to improve in any other respect."

Campaign Finance Reform Is Necessary

Elizabeth Drew

An increasing number of elected officials and observers of government claim that the political process is being distorted by the continuous fund-raising required to stay in office. In the following viewpoint, Elizabeth Drew, Washington correspondent for *The New Yorker*, argues that reform of the campaign financing process is necessary to keep elected officials answerable to the voters and not just to special interests that finance their campaigns.

As you read, consider the following questions:

1. According to the author, why haven't the campaign finance reforms enacted in 1974 decreased the influence of big donors?
2. How does Drew think the pressure to raise campaign funds affects who decides to run for office?
3. Why does Drew believe that reliance on special interest money distorts the legislative process?

Reprinted with permission of Macmillan Publishing Company from *Politics and Money* by Elizabeth Drew. Copyright © 1983 by Elizabeth Drew.

The role that money is currently playing in American politics is different both in scope and in nature from anything that has gone before. The acquisition of campaign funds has become an obsession on the part of nearly every candidate for federal office. The obsession leads the candidates to solicit and accept money from those most able to provide it, and to adjust their behavior in office to the need for money—and the fear that a challenger might be able to obtain more. There are ostensible limits on how much can be contributed to candidates for the House and the Senate, but those limits are essentially meaningless. The law that established public financing of Presidential campaigns was intended to remove the role of private money from Presidential contests, but great rivers of private money, much of it untraceable, still flow into them. The only limits on how much money can be directed toward the election of a President are those on ingenuity.

Reforms Are Amusing

The 1974 law setting limits on contributions to congressional and Presidential campaigns and establishing public financing for Presidential elections was finally enacted, after years of effort, amid the uproar over Watergate, when it was revealed that large, illegal corporate contributions had gone toward the election of Richard Nixon in 1972, that individuals had contributed enormous sums—the champion being W. Clement Stone, who contributed more than two million dollars—and that ambassadorships had been awarded to large contributors. But under the new laws there is nothing to prevent a W. Clement Stone from contributing a vast sum of money for the election of a Presidential candidate; he would simply have to go to more trouble to do so. A number of people did just that in the 1980 election. And ambassadorships and other high positions are still awarded to large contributors and fund raisers. The laws have given rise to "independent" committees working on a Presidential candidate's behalf which are independent in name only.

The political practitioners who have learned their way around both the Presidential and the congressional campaign-finance laws—and all the skilled ones have—view them with amusement. One Democratic practitioner says, "They are over-regulating the penguins on the tip of the iceberg." One Republican practitioner says the idea that there are any limits on the amounts of money that can flow into a Presidential campaign is "a myth." One oil lobbyist says that the idea that the law requiring the disclosure of funds contributed to congressional campaigns gives a real picture of the sources of the funds is "a joke." Senator Daniel Inouye, Democrat of Hawaii, says, "I think we're back about where we were before the laws were passed."

The result of all this is that the basis on which our system of representative government was supposed to work is slipping away, if it is not already gone. The role of the public representative has been changing dramatically in recent years. The processes by which Congress is supposed to function have been distorted, if not overwhelmed, by the role of money. The ability of even the best of the legislators to focus on broad questions, to act independently, or to lead has been seriously impaired. The race for money on Capitol Hill has turned into what one House member has described as "a fever" that has taken over the institution. The nature of the kind of person who might enter national politics is changing. Politicians who seek to enter, and do not have great wealth of their own to spend, are signed up on a systematic basis by interests that wish to enjoy influence over their official conduct. Many estimable people are concluding that they would prefer not to enter at all.

A Corrosive Problem

I am concerned because one basic problem is undermining the ability of Congress to address any other issues effectively. That problem is the corrosive, pervasive, and too often invisible influence of special interest money. Most damaging to the Congress is the recent explosion in campaign contributions from political action committees (PACs), which are formed by corporations, unions, trade associations, and ideological groups in order to exercise influence by contributing money to election campaigns. There are other forms of special interest money, however, that are also increasingly corroding the integrity of Congress, such as speaking fees, known as honoraria, and the undisclosed, multimillion-dollar lobbying efforts of various industries and interest groups.

Richard Bolling, *The Annals of the American Academy of Political and Social Science*, July 1986.

The Washington lobbyists and political consultants understand what is going on, and so do the politicians. "The key thing," says one lobbyist, "is what all this is doing to the way we govern ourselves. I think we're reaching the point where legislators make decisions only after thinking about what this means in terms of the money that will come to them or go to their opponents." A young lawyer-lobbyist says, "If you went into a typical senator's or congressman's office a few years ago, almost no one knew who the contributors were or who was coming to the fund-raisers. Now almost every staff member is involved: everybody is asked to give money, to get people to give money, to work on the fund-raising. The fact is that money is everything on the Hill these days. The change is overwhelming. When you talk to someone on Capitol Hill, inevitably the conversation turns to how much money the member has raised, where he's getting it, where he can get more." A Washington lawyer says, "Fund-raising has become a continuous activity."

Through the nineteen-fifties, everyone knew that sums of cash were in circulation, in exchange for legislation. The Bobby Baker scandal was just a symptom. The difference between then and now is one of approach and extent. Says a former Capitol Hill aide, "Now the politicians need more and more money; therefore, their threshold of principle is lower, and their willingness to compromise is greater. Everyone has learned that this is the way to do business." A number of members of Congress say they fear that some great scandal about money may be about to explode. In fact, that scandal may already be occurring. It takes the form not of one explosive event but of many often undramatic, everyday events. The search for one particular scandal misses the point. It is analogous to the search for the "smoking gun" during Watergate—the one clear example of criminality—in a landscape strewn with evidence of abuse of power.

Law-Making Process Distorted

The federal criminal statute makes it a crime to give or promise, or to ask for or receive, "anything of value" in exchange for any official act. The transactions between donors and politicians may stop short of such explicitness—though sometimes they do not— but the people involved in such transactions know the codes for getting around the letter, not to mention the spirit, of the law. Of course, not every contribution comes with a due bill, and not every politician is incapable of accepting a contribution and exercising independent judgment. And many contributions are made because the contributor already agrees with the candidate's point of view. But the pressures to gather large amounts of money are so great that the legislative process is inherently distorted, even corrupted, by the phenomenon. The effect of money on the legislative process takes several forms, some of them seemingly, but not actually, contradictory, and many, if not most, of them hidden from view. Because of the need for money or the fear of a well-financed opponent, a member of Congress might vote a certain way on a piece of legislation, or might try to avoid a vote on the matter, or might even forestall congressional consideration of it altogether. The effect might be in some action in a subcommittee, or some message to a colleague, that does not come to light. Legislation that in the earlier years might not have ever been seriously considered but has the backing of a particularly well-financed interest group can go whizzing through Congress. Other legislation, often involving important issues, can be so caught in the tangle of competing interests that Congress is paralyzed.

Until the problem of money is dealt with, it is unrealistic to expect the political process to improve in any other respect. It is not relevant whether every candidate who spends more than his opponent wins—though in races that are otherwise close, this tends to be the case. What matters is what the chasing of money does to the candidates, and to the victors' subsequent behavior. The candidates' desperation for money and the interests' desire to affect public policy provide a mutual opportunity. The issue is not how much is spent on elections but the way the money is obtained.

Money, Money, Money

I know something about how Senators have to go out and spend their time in this grubby, demeaning task of trying to raise money for their reelection campaigns. They are forced to do it by necessity.

They are simply facing up to the realities of the era in which we live, the electronic age—computers, media consultants, expensive mailing lists, all of these things. But they have to do it. It is a case of survival. Self-survival is one of the first laws of nature and they are being forced to engage in this unceasing, ever-increasing demand for money, money, money—the money chase.

I am concerned that if something is not done about it, we are going to see things go from bad to worse, and the faith and confidence and trust that the people should accord to this institution, the legislative branch, are going to be undermined, eroded, and that will result in lasting injury to this institution that we all love.

Robert Byrd, *The Congressional Digest*, February 1987.

The argument made by some that the amount spent on campaigns is not particularly bothersome, because it comes to less than is spent on, say, advertising cola, or purchasing hair-care products, misses the point stunningly. The point is what *raising* money, not simply spending it, does to the political process. It is not just that the legislative product is bent or stymied. It is not just that well-armed interests have a head start over the rest of the citizenry—or that often it is not even a contest. It is not just that citizens without organized economic power pay the bill for the successes of those with organized economic power. It is not even relevant which interests happen to be winning. What is relevant is what the whole thing is doing to the democratic process. What is at stake is the idea of representative government, the soul of this country.

VIEWPOINT

2

"*Campaign reform would cure problems that don't exist with solutions that would restrict free speech, smother elections . . . and hurt candidates' chances of beating incumbents.*"

Campaign Finance Reform Is Not Necessary

Robert J. Samuelson

Critics of campaign finance reform argue that efforts to control the influence of special interests on campaigns are misguided. In the following viewpoint, Robert J. Samuelson, a columnist with *Newsweek* magazine, claims that the special interest money has always been a part of democratic government, and that its corrupting influence is exaggerated.

As you read, consider the following questions:

1. Why does Samuelson believe that the increasing amount of money used in campaigns does not corrupt elected officials?
2. What evidence does the author give that the harmful influence of political action committees is exaggerated?
3. Why does Samuelson believe that in restricting campaign finance, reformers are limiting freedom of speech?

Robert J. Samuelson, "The Campaign Reform Fraud." From *Newsweek*, July 13, 1987. © 1987, Newsweek, Inc. All rights reserved. Reprinted by permission.

The Founding Fathers are growling in their graves. The Senate is now debating campaign-finance "reform": a respectable-sounding idea that's a fraud. Campaign reform would cure problems that don't exist with solutions that would restrict free speech, smother elections in bureaucratic rules and hurt candidates' chances of beating incumbents. It's an odd way to celebrate the Constitution's 200th birthday.

Special Interests Inevitable

Blame that on Fred Wertheimer of Common Cause. His crusade for reform—campaign-spending restrictions and public financing—is built on half-truths. He says that campaign contributions of "special interests" have corrupted politics. They haven't. The Founding Fathers knew that special interests were inevitable. Their government of checks and balances requires compromise; competing groups check each other. The system isn't perfect, but it curbs the undue influence of campaign contributors.

Wertheimer is a genius at obscuring this. He harps on the huge rise in congressional campaign spending—up from $195 million in 1978 to $450 million in 1986—and its simplest implication: because congressmen need more money, they're more beholden to donors. The obvious answer is to limit dependence on the donors. The logic fits popular prejudices about special interests, and most editorialists and journalists accept Common Cause's claims uncritically. They shouldn't.

For starters, money doesn't determine who wins elections. Winning candidates are often outspent. In . . . [the 1986] Senate election, says political scientist Michael Malbin, six of the seven Democrats who ousted incumbent Republicans were outspent by an average of about 75 percent. There are too many other influences to make money decisive: the economy, party loyalties, personalities, issues, national mood. The 1986 election results, Brooks Jackson of *The Wall Street Journal* wrote later, suggested "that much . . . money was spent with little practical effect."

Bias Against Challengers

Paradoxically, campaign reform could make it tougher for challengers to unseat incumbents. If money doesn't settle elections, serious challengers need adequate minimums to gain name recognition and project campaign themes. It's these threshold amounts that campaign reform threatens. The spending limits in the bill before the Senate are below what five of the winning Senate Democratic challengers spent. In North Carolina, Terry Sanford spent $4.17 million to beat former senator James T. Broyhill. The bill would have allowed Sanford $2.95 million.

No one is smart enough to set "correct" spending limits based on population or anything else. States and congressional districts differ radically in political characteristics. California races require lots of media spending. That's less true in Chicago. Spending in hotly contested races is typically higher than average. Because Congress—that is, incumbents—would control spending limits, the bias would be against challengers.

Likewise, Wertheimer's assertion that campaign contributions corrupt the legislative process is similarly weak. You hear lots of talk about the dangers of political-action committees (PAC's). What you don't hear is:

- PAC's remain a minority of all contributions. In 1986 they were 21 percent for the Senate (up from 17 percent in 1984) and 34 percent for the House (level with 1984).
- The diversity of the 4,157 PAC's dilutes their power. There are business PAC's, labor PAC's, pro-abortion PAC's, anti-abortion PAC's, importer PAC's and protectionist PAC's. Contributions are fairly evenly split between Democrats ($74.6 million in 1986) and Republicans ($57.5 million).
- PAC's give heavily to senior, powerful congressmen, who are politically secure and not easily intimidated. According to Common Cause, Democratic Rep. Augustus Hawkins of California is the most dependent on PAC contributions (92 percent). First elected in 1962, he won last year with 85 percent of the vote.

Abandon All Limits

As long as the cost of running a race keeps rising, parties and candidates will do whatever it takes to get around any limits regulators dream up. It's far from clear that we'd be worse-off under a system where one wealthy, yet principled, individual could single-handedly bankroll a candidate. More important, it's hard to square limits on contributions and spending with the First Amendment. Since we agree with the Court that people ought to be able to spend as much money as they want promoting their beliefs, we think it's time to abandon all limits, and with them the tortured distinction between expenditures and contributions. Let the fat cats give all they want— with full, detailed public disclosure of all spending and contributions to guard against abuse.

The New Republic, December 1, 1986.

Of course special interests mob Congress. That's democracy. One person's special interest is another's crusade or livelihood. To be influential, people organize. As government's powers have grown, so has lobbying by affected groups: old people, farmers, doctors, teachers. The list runs on. But PAC's are only a minor influence on voting. Political scientist Frank Sorauf of the University of Minnesota reports that in 1984 the average PAC contribution to House incumbents was less than one-third of 1 percent of the average congressman's total receipts. Congressmen vote according to their political views, constituents' interests, party wishes and—yes—their consciences. Special interests were supposed to block tax reform. They didn't.

Open and Freewheeling

About half the rise in campaign spending since 1978 reflects inflation. Much of the rest stems from the emergence of younger politicians who use expensive campaign consultants, television and direct mail. In 1984 Democratic House Speaker Thomas P. O'Neill Jr. of Massachusetts spent $213,000 winning re-election. In 1986 Democrat Joseph P. Kennedy II spent $1.8 million to win the same seat. But the expense of modern communications makes it no less vital for free speech.

That's why the Supreme Court held in 1976 that mandatory campaign-spending limits on candidates violate the First Amendment. Public financing of election spending aims to make "voluntary" limits more acceptable. But even if voluntary limits on candidates were enacted, the problem of "independent spending" remains: if I want to buy TV time to support Joe Blow, the Supreme Court says that's my right. Candidate spending limits would prompt special interests to raise independent spending. The Senate bill tries to deter this by subsidizing responses: my $10,000 praising Joe Blow would entitle his opponent to $10,000 of public money to answer me.

Suppose this were judged constitutional (unlikely), what's the point? In our diverse society, one role of politics is to allow the venting of different opinions and pent-up frustrations. Groups need to feel they can express themselves and participate without colliding with obtuse rules intended to shut them out. Our politics is open and freewheeling. Its occasional excesses are preferable to arbitrary restraints. Wertheimer's brand of reform is misconceived. The Senate would dignify the Founding Fathers by rejecting it.

"The PAC [Political Action Committee] system is a rotten system that must be changed."

Political Action Committees Are Too Powerful

Fred Wertheimer

Political Action Committees [PACs] are groups set up by corporations, unions, and other organizations to collect contributions from individuals and distribute them to political candidates. In the following viewpoint, Fred Wertheimer argues that PACs play too large of a role in financing election campaigns and that PAC sponsors have undue influence over the decisions of elected officials. He is the president of Common Cause, a citizens' lobbying organization.

As you read, consider the following questions:

1. According to Wertheimer, what crucial step did Congress fail to take when it passed legislation regulating PACs?
2. What reasons does the author give for not believing the claim that PACs allow for more citizen involvement in politics?
3. According to the US senators quoted by Wertheimer, what negative influence do PACs have on congressional decision making?

Fred Wertheimer, "Campaign Finance Reform: The Unfinished Agenda," *The Annals of the American Academy of Political and Social Science,* Vol. 486 (July 1986), pp. 87, 90-94, 102. Copyright © 1986 by The American Academy of Political and Social Science. Reprinted by permission of Sage Publications, Inc.

Our democracy is founded on the concept of representation. Citizens elect leaders who are given responsibility to weigh all the competing and conflicting interests that reflect our diversity and to decide what, in their judgment, will best advance the interests of the citizenry.

It is obviously a rough system. It often does not measure up to the ideal we might hope to attain. But we continue to place our trust in this system because we believe our best chance at governing ourselves lies in obtaining the best judgment of elected representatives.

Violating Democratic Values

Unfortunately, that is not happening today. We are not obtaining the best judgment of our elected representatives in Congress because they are not free to give it to us. As a result of our present congressional campaign financing system—and the increasing role of political action committee (PAC) campaign contributions—members of Congress are rapidly losing their ability to represent the constituencies that have elected them. . . .

Congress and PACs

The last decade of congressional campaign financing has been marked by an exponential increase in the number of PACs formed by corporations, labor unions, trade associations, and other groups. In 1974 there were 608 PACs. Today there are more than 4000.

This explosion in PACs can be traced to congressional action— and inaction— in 1974. Ironically, at the very time when members of Congress were acting to clean up presidential elections, they opened the door for PACs to enter the congressional arena in an unprecedented way. The key to the PAC explosion was a provision attached to the 1974 law by labor and business groups, over the opposition of Common Cause and other reform advocates, that authorized government contractors to establish PACs. In addition, by creating public financing for presidential campaigns, but not for congressional races, the 1974 amendments focused the attention and interest of PACs and other private campaign donors on Congress.

The resulting growth in PACs was no accident, and it certainly was not a reform. The growth of PACs, moreover, is certainly no unintended consequence of the 1974 law—the provision was included to protect and enhance the role of PACs in financing campaigns, and it has.

This tremendous increase in the number of PACs has not resulted in balanced representation in Washington. As [former] Senator Gary Hart, Democrat of Colorado, has told the Senate:

> It seems the only group without a well-heeled PAC is the average citizen—the voter who has no special interest beyond low taxes, an efficient government, an honorable Congress, and

Ed Gamble. Reprinted with permission.

a humane society. Those are the demands we should be heeding—but those are the demands the PACs have drowned out.

In fact, the increasing number of PACs has largely served to increase the ability of single interests to bring pressure to bear on a congressional candidate or a member of Congress. There are more than 100 insurance company PACs, more than 100 PACs sponsored by electric utilities, and more than 300 sponsored by labor unions. Representative David Obey, Democrat of Wisconsin, has observed that frequently in Washington

> an issue affects an entire industry and all of the companies and labor unions in that industry. . . . When that occurs, [and] a large number of groups which have made substantial contributions to members are all lobbying on the same side of an issue, the pressure generated from those aggregate contributions is enormous and warps the process. It is as if they had made a single, extremely large contribution.

The increase in the number of PACs, not surprisingly, has also produced a tremendous increase in PAC contributions to congressional candidates. In 1974, PACs gave $12.5 million to congressional candidates. By the 1984 elections, their contributions had exceeded $100 million, an eightfold increase in ten years.

PAC money also represents a far more important part of the average candidate's campaign funds than it did ten or so years ago. In 1974, 15.7 percent of congressional candidates' campaign money came from PACs; by the 1984 election, that proportion had increased to 30 percent.

Money Goes to Winner

Yet these numbers only begin to tell the story. The increased dependence on PAC contributions has been greatest for winners, those individuals who serve in Congress and who cast votes that shape our daily lives. In the Ninety-ninth Congress (1985-86), over 150 House members received 50 percent or more of their campaign funds from PACs, including 20 of the 27 committee chairs and party leaders. House winners in the 1984 election received an average of 41 percent of their campaign dollars from PACs. Of all winning House candidates in the 1974 election, only 28 percent received one-third or more of their campaign funds from PACs. By 1984, that figure had grown to 78 percent.

For senators, PAC contributions are also becoming a more important source of campaign dollars. Senators elected in 1976 received a total of $3.1 million from PACs; Senate winners in the 1984 election raised $20 million from PACs. In the 1984 elections, 23 winning Senate candidates raised more than $500,000 each from PACs.

Some have suggested that the growth in PACs is an important new form of citizen involvement in the political process. Yet PAC participation is often likely to be more of an involvement in the corporate process or the union process or the trade association process than it is in the political process. University of Minnesota professor Frank J. Sorauf has noted:

> To understand political participation through PACs, we need also to note the nature of the participation. Some of it is not even political activity; buying a ticket in a raffle, the proceeds of which go to a PAC, a party, or a candidate, does not qualify as a political act by most standards. Even the contributory act of writing a check or giving cash to a PAC is a somewhat limited form of participation that requires little time or immediate involvement; in a sense it buys political mercenaries who free the contributor from the need to be personally active in the campaign. It is one of the least active forms of political activity, well suited to the very busy or to those who find politics strange, boring, or distasteful.

PACs Help Incumbents, Contributors

In fact, the growth of PACs and the increased importance of PAC money have had a negative effect on two different parts of the political process—congressional elections and congressional decision making. First, PAC money tends to make congressional campaigns less competitive because of the overwhelming advantage enjoyed by incumbents in PAC fund-raising. The ratio of PAC contributions to incumbents over challengers in 1984 House races was 4.6 to 1.00; in the Senate, incumbents in 1984 enjoyed a 3.0 to 1.0 advantage in PAC receipts. On the average, 1984 House incumbents raised $100,000 more from PACs than did challengers. This $100,000 advantage was true even in the most highly competitive House races, those in which the incumbent received 55 percent or less of the vote. In these races, incumbents received an average of over $230,000 from PACs; their challengers received less than $110,000. The advantage enjoyed by incumbents is true for all kinds of PAC giving—for contributions by labor groups, corporate PACs, and trade and membership PACs.

Fundamentally Corrupt

When Common Cause recently examined the financing of the seven Senate races in which Democratic challengers defeated Republican incumbents, it found 150 cases in which PACs backed the loser during the campaign, then supported the winner after the election.

Perhaps no other practice so convincingly establishes the fraudulence of claims that PACs are merely a means to coordinate contributions from well-intentioned citizens. . . .

The post-election contributions, cynically known among Washington insiders as "get-smart-late money," are only one manifestation of a system of financing elections for the House and Senate that is fundamentally corrupt.

There is no more abusive element of that system than the pervasive influence of PACs operated to advance the political agendas of special-interest groups.

Robert Walters, *The Washington Times*, April 30, 1987.

Second, there is a growing awareness that PAC money makes a difference in the legislative process, a difference that is inimical to our democracy. PAC dollars are given by special interest groups to gain special access and special influence in Washington. Most often, PAC contributions are made with a legislative purpose in mind. The late Justin Dart, former chairman of Dart Industries, once noted that dialogue with politicians "is a fine thing, but with a little money they hear you better." [Former] Senator Charles Mathias, Republican of Maryland, has stated:

An official may not change his or her vote solely to accommodate the views of such contributors, but often officials, including myself, will agree to meet with an individual who made a large contribution so the official can hear the contributor's concerns and make the contributor aware these concerns have been considered. . . . Since an elected official has only so much time available, the inevitable result of such special treatment for the large contributor is that other citizens are denied the opportunity they otherwise would have to confer with the elected official. Common Cause and others have produced a number of studies that show a relationship between PAC contributions and legislative behavior. The examples run the gamut of legislative decisions, including hospital cost containment, the Clean Air Act, domestic content legislation, dairy price programs, gun control, maritime policies, and regulation by the Federal Trade Commission of professional groups or of used-car sales.

Polluting the System

PAC gifts do not guarantee votes or support. PACs do not always win. But PAC contributions do provide donors with critical access and influence; they do affect legislative decisions and are increasingly dominating and paralyzing the legislative process.

In the last few years, something very important and fundamental has happened in this country—and that is the development of a growing awareness and recognition of the fact that the PAC system is a rotten system that must be changed. We know that concern is growing when Irving Shapiro, former chairman and chief executive officer of duPont and the former chairman of the Business Roundtable, describes the current system of financing congressional campaigns as ''an invidious thing, it's corrupting, it does pollute the system.'' . . .

Criticism of the PAC system is also increasingly heard in the halls of Congress. More and more members from both parties are speaking out about the PAC problem. Consider the following [statements by US senators]:

[The present campaign-financing system] virtually forces members of Congress to go around hat in hand, begging for money from Washington-based special interest political action committees, whose sole purpose for existing is to seek a quid pro quo. . . . [T]he scandal is taking place every day and will continue to do so while the present system is in place.

PAC money is destroying the election process. It is breaking down public confidence in free elections and it is ruining the character and quality of campaigns.

In addition, the growth in the influence of PAC's further fragments our Nation and its elected legislative bodies. It makes it increasingly difficult to reach a national consensus and hold[s] our decision-making process hostage to the special interests which PAC's represent. . . . We cannot expect Members of Congress to act in the national interest when their election campaigns are being financed more and more by special interests.

Skyrocketing Costs

In addition to the growing role of PAC contributions, the congressional campaign-financing system is also marked by unlimited and skyrocketing spending. In 1974, House and Senate candidates spent $77 million on congressional races. Ten years later, House and Senate candidates spent a record $374 million, almost five times as much.

The cost of winning a seat in Congress is also rising dramatically. In the 1975-76 election cycle, House winners spent $38 million, an average of over $87,000 each. In the 1983-84 election cycle, House winners spent $117 million, an average of $269,956 each. On the Senate side, winners spent $20 million in the 1975-76 cycle, an average of $606,060; in 1984 elections, Senate winners spent $94.8 million, an average of $2.9 million each. . . .

Conclusion

A consensus has been reached in this country that PACs are inimical to our system of representative government. The question now remaining is whether that public consensus can be translated into congressional action.

Best Congress Money Can Buy

Even if a Congressman or Senator can say in all sincerity that he or she isn't influenced by the tens of thousands of dollars taken in PAC money, the public is fully justified in believing that they have not necessarily elected the best Congress—but merely the best Congress that money can buy. . . .

We all know of the need for reform of our campaign finance system. The most precious heritage that we have in America is our democratic system of government. It is the envy of all the world, and has been the model for many other nations. But our democratic system is slowly being corroded and eroded by the influence of PAC money. As the amount of PAC money increases, our credibility and our appearance of integrity decreases.

John Kerry, *The Congressional Digest*, February 1987.

No solution that may be adopted will be final and perfect. We will always need to reevaluate and adjust any campaign finance system. The presidential public financing system demonstrates the need for periodic adjustments. But more important, the experience of presidential public financing shows us that fundamental improvement in our campaign finance laws is indeed attainable.

We can and must have a better system for financing congressional campaigns. Representative government is at stake.

"*[Political Action Committees] are the best way for the average citizen to participate in the process of self-government.*"

Political Action Committees Are Not Too Powerful

Phyllis Schlafly

Supporters of political action committees [PACs] claim that PACs allow individuals to have more access to the political process. The small contributions of many people can be pooled through PACs so that their contributions on behalf of a particular cause can make a difference. In the following viewpoint, Phyllis Schlafly argues that criticism of PACs is based on ideological prejudice, not a desire to make the electoral process more fair. Schlafly is a prominent conservative author and the founder and president of the Eagle Forum, a conservative activist group.

As you read, consider the following questions:

1. Why, according to Schlafly, are liberals against PACs?
2. According to the author, how do PACs make the electoral process more open?
3. Why does Schlafly think that the increasing amount of money spent on campaigns is not a problem?

Phyllis Schlafly, "PACs Protect Personal Political Participation," *The Phyllis Schlafly Report*, August 1986. Reprinted with the author's permission.

The liberals do not like PACs (Political Action Committees). That's because more Americans contribute through PACs toward the election of conservative candidates than liberal candidates. So the liberal busybodies have devised a three-point plan to out-maneuver democracy in order to advantage their candidates. (1) Get their liberal friends in the media to publish endless "news" stories, features, interviews with prominent persons, and editorials complaining about the large amounts of money donated through PACs. This is designed to have the subliminal effect of convincing people that PACs are something evil.

(2) Pass legislation severely restricting the amounts of money that PACs and political candidates may receive and spend. Label this legislation a "reform" or a "clean campaign" bill and hope that this semantic trick will expedite passage. . . .

(3) Bring about taxpayer financing of elections to replace voluntary financing of elections through PACs. In other words, make the taxpayers pay for what the PACs are paying for now.

Campaign Chicanery

It's quite an exercise in campaign chicanery to try to force citizens to finance the political campaigns of candidates they don't like, while prohibiting citizens from making voluntary contributions to the political campaigns of candidates they do like. In the peculiar inverted ideology of the liberals, it is bad for American citizens to spend $100 million of their own money on candidates of their own choice, but it would be good for the Federal Government to tax you and spend a similar amount of your money to elect candidates most of whom are not your choice.

It's quite a demonstration of the liberal dialectic to try to restrict First Amendment rights for political speech, while at the same time the entire liberal apparatus is working overtime to try to extend First Amendment rights for pornographic speech. One gets the feeling that, if PACs were promoting pornography instead of personal political views, the liberals might be supporting PACs.

In any event, it is vastly more important to the maintenance of our freedom to protect political than pornographic speech and activity. The First Amendment was written to protect political speech in order to retain our individual right to elect candidates and choose policies in a free society. PACs are simply one manifestation of your personal First Amendment right to express your political beliefs and to participate in the political process.

PACs Are Part of the Process

What are PACs? PACs are campaign committees set up by like-minded individuals to donate money to the candidates of their choice. They are the best way for the average citizen to participate in the process of self-government because they enable each of us to "put our money where our mouth is." There is nothing wrong with American citizens organizing and pooling their funds to make their legislative and political choices better known and more effective. That's what self-government is all about.

Those who want to restrict PACs complain that campaigning now costs too much. Sure, it costs more than it used to, but so does everything else. A candidate's ability to raise funds is a clear indication of his appeal to the voters. If he can't raise enough money to mount a campaign, it means that not enough voters care enough about his candidacy to help him get elected.

Ponder a moment on the fact that there is NO limit to the value of contributions that can be made to political candidates by the big corporations which operate newspapers and magazines. They can effectively contribute an unlimited amount to the candidates of their choice by publishing favorable news stories and features, as well as editorials, about candidates of their choice, along with negative items (or the silent treatment) about candidates they oppose.

Limiting PACs Helps Incumbents

Legislation to limit PAC contributions further—particularly legislation limiting the aggregate amount candidates may accept from PACs—might cause more problems than it would solve. In the face of rising campaign costs and the unlikely prospect that a budget-conscious Congress would enact compensatory legislation providing for public funding as an alternative source of money, such legislation would make it more difficult for candidates, especially challengers, to conduct competitive campaigns. Recent research has found that any increase in campaign funds generally helps challengers more than incumbents. To limit PAC giving would make it more difficult for challengers to mount effective campaigns and would increase the power of incumbents, who begin their reelection campaigns with notable advantages: the ability to command greater media attention than most challengers and allowances for salary, staff, travel, office, and communications worth about $1 million over a two-year term. And it would disadvantage candidates running against wealthy opponents spending large amounts of their own funds.

Herbert Alexander, *Financing Politics,* 1984.

Newspapers can even accept the paid advertisements of candidates they want to help, and refuse to print the paid advertisements of candidates they want to defeat. That's called "freedom of the press," and there are no limits on it. The dollar value of this type of contribution is vast and there is no way to measure it.

PACs enable the individual American, who doesn't own a newspaper or magazine, television or radio station, to participate effectively in the political process. Since the media enjoy such enormous power to support the candidates of their choice, it comes with exceedingly poor grace for any newspapers to try to restrict private individuals from making their voluntary contributions to the candidates of their choice.

Instead of editorializing against the rights of American voters to exercise their full First Amendment rights to contribute to political candidates, it would be more helpful to the political process if newspapers would publish the list of all those who contribute $1,000 or more to each candidate in the newspaper's Congressional district. Full disclosure, not limitation, is the best remedy for potential abuses.

PACs Around a Long Time

The first PAC was formed in 1943 by the CIO [Congress of Industrial Organizations]. For three decades the unions had a practical monopoly on PACs; unions made huge political contributions to candidates who voted for union-backed legislation.

When the majority of PAC money came from unions, we didn't hear any propaganda from the press and self-righteous liberal lobbies about how terrible PACs are. It's only since conservatives discovered that they, too, can have PACs that the liberals are upset.

The proliferation of PACs in the last ten years is the direct result of the Watergate "reform" laws. Funny thing, though, the 1974 election laws didn't have anything to do with the abuses of Watergate or the prosecutions that followed it.

The Federal Election Laws were passed in a euphoric effort to eliminate "corruption." Corruption may be important in the political games played at the local level in some parts of the country, but it was not the issue in Watergate. It is the least of the problems we have with politics in the Federal Government.

When the laws about political contributions, limitations, and disclosure were spelled out, then corporations, associations, and organizations suddenly discovered that they, too, could be financially active in politics.

Today, union PACs are contributing more than ever, but it is only one-fourth of the PAC money that flows into Congress, instead of 90 percent. The anti-PAC argument really is: if the majority of PAC money is conservative rather than liberal, then PACs must be bad.

Why Liberals Hate PACs

The real explanation for liberal antagonism to PACs was inadvertently revealed by Irvin Ross in the July 1983 *Reader's Digest* in the course of an impassioned plea for taxpayer financing of Congressional elections. He admitted that the liberals outsmarted themselves in their election "reform" legislation passed after Watergate.

What Ross called a "surprising development" was that conservatives began to use the 1974 law and set up dozens of PACs. From the 1940s to 1974, PACs were operated almost exclusively by labor unions, but Ross said that, by the time of his article, labor unions operated only 380 of 3,371 PACs.

PACs Get a Bum Rap

Although they are hardly perfect, in some ways PAC's have gotten a bum rap. In fact, they are the product of earlier reforms, and a real improvement over earlier fundraising practices. I have called PAC's the "united way of political giving" and I meant it. Consider the situation before 1974. At that time, campaign finance all too often was the province of a few big corporations and wealthy fatcats, who found ways to give nearly unlimited amounts of campaign funds with little or no disclosure.

In contrast, PAC's allow average citizens and small contributors to pool their resources and get involved in the political process. In fact, PAC's can act as a sort of half-way house to parties as a means of getting citizens involved in the process of self-government. People who donate to PAC's are more active, knowledgeable, and interested in the political process than the average citizen. And it's all done in the open, above board, with full disclosure.

David Durenberger, *The Congressional Digest*, February 1987.

Ross concluded: "Clearly, we need to reform campaign financing" and control "the PAC problem" by substituting taxpayer financing. The only thing "clear" from Ross' argument is that he wants to substitute a liberal/federal control mechanism in elections instead of allowing the American people voluntarily to spend their own money as they choose.

It might sound like a bit of flamboyant rhetoric to say that voluntary PACs versus taxpayer financing of Congressional candidates is an issue of freedom versus socialism, but that is substantially what a prominent liberal, Senator Eugene McCarthy, has said. He admitted that there is "a kind of socialist ideology that runs through a lot of the liberal movement." He said that many liberals think, "Why don't we have government control the political process?"

McCarthy, an outspoken defender of our full First Amendment rights to make political contributions, has given us some good advice about his liberal friends. He said, "When liberals turn reformers, beware. Dr. Guillotine's invention was welcomed by the reformers of the French Revolution. It was new, scientific, fast, clean, certain, and its side effects were minimal."

McCarthy added, "When liberals become reformers, you're in

deep trouble—like the second stage of the French Revolution." He compares liberal reformers to the Robespierre liberals who supported the guillotine because it was more humane than the older method of executions by axe; the guillotine also diffused responsibility since gravity rather than a human hand delivered the fatal blow.

The anti-PAC liberal reformers are trying to persuade the taxpayers to assume the responsibility for electing candidates to Congress so you will never know whom to blame when you don't like how the money is spent. The best way to keep Congressional elections "clean" is to keep them as far away as possible from government control and taxpayer financing.

Advocacy Journalism Against PACs

The lobby called Common Cause is leading the pack against PACs. Common Cause wants to restrict your right to help elect candidates so that Common Cause, through its big mailing list, can exert more influence over the Congressmen who are elected.

A steady drumbeat of anti-PAC newspaper articles and editorials always accelerates in the weeks before an anti-PAC bill is due to come up in the Congress. . . . The *New York Times* professes indignation that there are now 4,000 PACs raising campaign contributions and pouring $100 million a year into Congressional campaigns.

So what! All that money was voluntary. Nobody forced anybody to contribute to PACs or to accept money from a PAC. Americans spend only $1 on PACs for every $75 they spend on tobacco, and only $1 on PACs for every $231 they spend on alcohol.

The $100 million spent voluntarily on PACs is much less than the $144 million the taxpayers were forced to spend to pay for mass mailings by Senators and Congressmen to their constituents, most of which are directly related to getting themselves reelected.

Most editorials on PACs start from the assumption that "everybody wants to cut down the enormous cost of political campaigns." That's false. Some of us think it's healthy that $100 million was voluntarily spent by American citizens as their investment in the public officials and public policies that the voters want. This is citizen participation in the process of self-government and the exercise of our First Amendment rights of free speech and assembly.

Voters Pooling Resources

Those who want to restrict PACs argue that, a decade ago, contributions under $100 made up nearly half of all the money given in Congressional races, and now it's only 19%, so that means "ordinary voters are squeezed out by the fat PACs." These figures don't mean that at all. They mean that voters who contribute less than $100 have found a way to pool their resources with other less-than-$100 contributors in order to let their voice be heard at the national level.

PACs cannot be blamed for inventing "special-interest groups." They always existed. In the pre-PAC era, their money was distributed in brown paper bags, or shoe boxes, or unmarked envelopes. By contrast, with PACs, we have full disclosure of all contributions, and extremely low limitations on contributions ($5,000 to any federal candidate in a single election). That's hardly enough to buy a 30-second TV spot.

Some of the anti-PAC rhetoric comes from the two major political parties because the average candidate now gets about three times as much money from PACs as from a political party. PACs have risen in influence as the parties diminished in their effectiveness in dealing with the issues that voters really care about.

Let's hear no more from those who complain that other Americans are giving their own hard-earned money to PACs. How could there be a more constructive way to spend money than to try to elect candidates who will give us the kind of government we want?

"Public financing in congressional campaigns would . . . give officeholders a greater measure of freedom to address issues in the broad national interest."

Taxpayers Should Finance Political Campaigns

Charles McC. Mathias Jr.

Candidates running for political offices must raise large amounts of money to put their messages and ideas before voters. In the following viewpoint, Charles McC. Mathias Jr. advocates giving federal tax dollars to political candidates. By doing this, Mathias believes, the government would free candidates and incumbents from the constant fund-raising that is now an essential part of holding office. Mathias is a former Republican senator from Maryland.

As you read, consider the following questions:

1. How would public financing of campaigns improve the election process, according to the author?
2. What characteristics of campaign financing will not be affected by public financing, according to Mathias?
3. Why does Mathias believe that public financing will not give unfair advantage to incumbents?

Charles McC. Mathias, "Should There Be Public Financing of Congressional Campaigns?" *The Annals of the American Academy of Political and Social Science,* July 1986.

Samuel Johnson once remarked that nothing is so conducive to a good conscience as the suspicion that someone may be watching.

This observation reminds us of the purpose and underlying principle of campaign finance reform. In a perfect world, there would be no need to proscribe certain behavior in the setting of political campaigns, since individuals would not seek influence through their contributions, candidates would never be beholden to large donors, and the system itself would remain an open one. In the real world, campaign finance laws are necessary rules of behavior designed to protect the political process and promote certain basic democratic values. These laws and their enforcement help ensure that elections and government itself are free of abuses that would subvert democratic society. . . .

Unfinished Business

The role of money in elections is a troubling spectacle to this nation. The first stages of reform have given us a great wealth of information on campaign finances, but the statistics also warn that the problems of big money in the process persist. The potential for abuse lingers on because of unfinished business: the Congress's failure to provide for public financing of congressional campaigns. . . .

Restoring Integrity

Partial public funding with realistic expenditure ceilings would enable candidates to run competitive campaigns in which private funding would continue to play an important but not a dominant role. A grant of public funds would free candidates from the incessant demands of fund-raising and offers the hope of shortening the seemingly endless campaign season. A system of public finance that includes a limit on the amount candidates may contribute to their own campaigns would eliminate the unfair advantage enjoyed by those with great personal wealth. And most important, public financing in congressional campaigns would restore a missing equilibrium between the sources of campaign funding and give officeholders a greater measure of freedom to address issues in the broad national interest. Such results would go a long way toward renewing public belief in the integrity of the electoral process.

Some will say that such further reforms will only lead to more creative means of circumventing the limits, that "special interest money has always found its way into the political system . . . [and] always will." All reform, however, is based on the notion that there are values at stake that make it worthwhile and, in some instances, imperative to control the potential for abuse in a system. That reforms at times have failed to achieve their stated goals, or that they have produced unintended and perhaps undesirable consequences, should not lead us to abandon efforts to safeguard the integrity of a process so vital to the preservation of democratic values. Perhaps as important as stating what public funding would do is stating what it would not do. The most serious concern is that publicly funded congressional campaigns, with limits on spending, would divert money into other channels—specifically, into independent expenditures. . . .

Regulating Independent Expenditures

Even if independent expenditures increased dramatically, we do not have to accept as inevitable that they would wreak havoc on the political system. Instead, we should ask what means exist for regulating independent expenditures, if they become a problem.

Get Them To Say "No"

I believe that the overwhelming majority of representatives and senators would more faithfully represent the interests of their constituents if they could afford to do so. Therefore we must look for ways to make it easier for them to say no to PACs, to say no to the interest groups offering honoraria, and to say no to hidden lobbying pressures. The best way we can help members of Congress say no is to provide some form of public financing of congressional campaigns. Although public financing of presidential campaigns has not been trouble free, and even though it also needs improvement, it has been undeniably successful in helping presidential candidates resist special interest money. Watergate demonstrated that, in 1972, the presidency was on the special interest auction block. By contrast, PAC money now accounts for less than 2 percent of presidential campaign funds. In fact, in the 1984 presidential contest, three candidates declared that they would not accept any PAC funds. We need to provide that kind of flexibility to members of Congress, and public financing is the best way to provide it.

Richard Bolling, *The Annals of the American Academy of Political and Social Science,* July 1986.

The Supreme Court, in striking down limits on independent expenditures in *Buckley* [v. *Valeo*], stated, "Independent advocacy . . . does not presently appear to pose dangers of real or apparent corruption comparable to those identified with large campaign contributions." Unfortunately, in a more recent case the Supreme Court again struck down limits on independent expenditures, holding unconstitutional a $1000 limit on independent spending by political committees in support of candidates in presidential general elections who accepted public funding. The Court in a 7-to-2 decision held that the expenditures in question were entitled to full First Amendment protection and, absent a showing of any "tendency . . . to corrupt or to give the appearance of corruption," the $1000 limit was constitutionally infirm. As Justice White notes in his dissent, the Court's continuing reluctance to defer to Congress in Congress's effort to regulate campaign finance remains a formidable barrier to achieving a system broadly designed, in his words, to "eliminate the danger of corruption, maintain public confidence in the integrity of federal elections, equalize the resources available to the candidates, and hold the overall amount of money devoted to political campaigning down to a reasonable level."

Are They Independent?

Even though the Supreme Court for the present appears unconvinced that there are compelling reasons for limiting independent spending, Congress can still take steps to curb the abuses associated with such spending. First, Congress should encourage rigorous enforcement of the requirement that there be no coordination with a candidate's campaign. Second, Congress should consider new legislative means of counteracting the harmful effects of independent expenditures in more direct ways.

A question to be considered at the outset is whether the independent expenditures are in compliance with existing law; that is, are they truly independent? Current law defines an independent expenditure as

an expenditure by a person expressly advocating the election or defeat of a clearly identified candidate which is made without cooperation or consultation with any candidate, or any authorized committee or agent of such candidate, and which is not made in concert with, or at the request or suggestion of, any candidate, or any authorized committee or agent of such candidate.

To the extent that these guidelines are observed, it was the Court's view at least that "independent expenditures may well provide little assistance to the candidate's campaign." It is still far from clear whether independent expenditures may be able to influence, let alone decide, election results. One of the largest independent expenditure committees, the National Conservative Political Action Committee (NCPAC), established its reputation in 1980 when four out of the six liberal Senate incumbents it targeted in its negative campaigning lost their reelection bids. In 1982, however, of nine targeted House and Senate candidates against whom NCPAC spent amounts ranging from $127,000 to $783,000, only one was defeated. NCPAC spent over $600,000 in the U.S. Senate race in Maryland in 1982 in a negative campaign that by most accounts helped the candidate it attacked and hurt his

"There has to be a better way to get there."

————from *Herblock At Large* (Pantheon 1987).

Republican opponent, who lost the election by a wide margin. That independent expenditures may be unpredictable in their effect and that in some instances they have backfired do not mean that they cannot have harmful consequences for the political process. If these occur, Congress should consider new legislation to address the problem.

Public Finance and Political Parties

The discussion of the consequences of public finance would be incomplete without asking what effect it would have on the political parties. In spite of early predictions, it is obvious that campaign finance regulation has not brought about the demise of the major parties. The Republican Party, in a way now being copied by the Democrats, has adapted remarkably well to both the law and the new technologies of campaigning. Within the constraints of contribution limits, the Republican National Committee, the National Republican Senatorial Committee, and the National Republican Congressional Committee have all been enormously successful fund-raisers, able to assist Republican candidates up to the maximum allowable limits under current law. Although parity does not now exist between the two major parties in fund-raising ability, it will no doubt come to pass before the decade is out.

Public funding need not affect the contributions and coordinated spending efforts parties are currently able to make on behalf of candidates. Ways of further expanding the parties' role might well be explored, both in the context of publicly funded congressional races and through other legislative proposals to encourage party-building efforts. As significant as the monetary contributions of parties are, considerable advantages flow from an ongoing organizational structure and a steadily growing body of expertise on effective campaign techniques. Some, in fact, see parties taking over many of the functions of political consultants in providing campaign services to candidates, a development that would further enhance the role of parties as formidable players in campaign finance.

Party Balance Stays the Same

Proposals for publicly funded campaigns also have raised the conflicting concerns that the major parties will face an onslaught of third-party and independent candidacies and that such a system will altogether freeze out candidacies from other than the major parties. Both fears seem exaggerated.

A system of public finance cannot constitutionally exclude independent and third-party candidates. Yet the concern that public finance would artificially bolster independent and third-party candidacies seems unwarranted. Virtually every public finance proposal discussed in Congress has imposed a threshold eligibility requirement. The requirement may consist of a specified amount of money that a candidate must raise in order to qualify for public funds or a certain number or percentage of signatures of qualified voters or of ballots cast in the election. To the extent that third-party candidates or independents are able to meet reasonable qualifying thresholds, they are entitled to some measure of public funding, a result that should not threaten the stability of the system. While public funding may to some extent stimulate fund-raising efforts or other activity by third-party candidates in order to qualify for public funds, it is difficult to see how a system of matching grants would radically change the amount of funds available to non-major-party candidates in the process.

Public Financing Encourages Competition

Two arguments made against public financing are that it would amount to an incumbent-protection act, since incumbents enjoy certain advantages, and that it would guarantee a challenger enough money to give an incumbent a disconcertingly stiff race. (The second argument is one that people on Capitol Hill make very quietly.) Both arguments, of course, can't be true. And if public financing amounted to an incumbent-protection act, it would have passed long since, unless Congress is an uncommonly noble institution. Moreover, most of the public-financing schemes have taken it into account that a highly restrictive spending limit would prevent challengers from competing effectively. Fred Wertheimer, the president of Common Cause, points out that the first two incumbent Presidents to run under the system of public financing of Presidential campaigns—Ford and Carter—both lost. As for the advantages of incumbency, Common Cause has brought legal action against abuse of the franking privilege. Wertheimer adds, "Incumbency has its pluses and its minuses." He says, "The key is to have a system that allows a challenger to compete. That's really all we can do, and that's all we should do."

Elizabeth Drew, *Politics and Money*, 1983.

Finally, a word should be said about the alleged pro-incumbent bias of public finance. This is a subject on which reasonable men and women have disagreed and probably will continue to do so. The most commonly heard argument is that expenditure limits are likely to hurt challengers more severely, since ordinarily they will need to spend more than an incumbent simply to achieve name recognition. A companion argument suggests that spending limits fail to take into account the considerable benefits accruing to an incumbent by virtue of the perquisites of office.

Does a challenger have to outspend an incumbent in order to win? The figures show that some challengers who outspent incumbents won and that, conversely, some who were outspent by the incumbents won. What may well be as important to a competitive race by a challenger is the certainty that an adequate level of funding will be available, to enable a challenger to develop his or her campaign strategy well in advance.

A lack of funds at a critical stage in a campaign can be devastating, and an abundance of funds so late in the campaign that planning opportunities have been lost can be of little use. The challenger who lacks funds early, for instance, cannot at the last minute produce and run television advertisements that may be crucial. In addition to improving opportunities for campaign management, public funding would introduce the concept of a level playing field in a large number of congressional races in which it would otherwise be absent—hardly a boon to incumbents.

There still may be the fear that public funding fails to take into account the obvious value of incumbency itself. Thus, in reality, challengers will be outspent in every race.

Liabilities of Incumbents

The official duties of members of Congress do encompass activities that can be factors in a member's reelection. Not the least of these is a member's voting record. The use of voting records in past campaigns suggests that this fact is not lost upon challengers or others. An incumbent's record alone may not cancel out the advantages of incumbency, but it should not be ignored when evaluating the fairness of a system of public finance.

The liabilities associated with incumbency do not justify an incumbent's using the resources of his or her office in patently political ways. Reforms undertaken by both houses of Congress in recent years reflect a concern that members of Congress not be perceived as using their position of public trust for political advantage. Ultimately, any system of public finance must take into account concerns about the advantages of incumbency and, if necessary, must include provisions to compensate challengers for such advantages. That such adjustments may be needed should not overshadow the many positive attributes of a system of publicly funded congressional elections.

Conclusion

Public funding of congressional races is a workable solution to the problems that are most troubling in the current system of campaign finance. The role money plays in elections has made it increasingly difficult for the democratic process to function properly. If we continue on our present course, eventually we will reach the day when the amassing and spending of campaign money will have fatally undermined public confidence in the process and thwarted the democratic values the system is supposed to serve.

"Taxpayer-financing [of elections] would protect incumbents from the public."

Taxpayers Should Not Finance Political Campaigns

Frank J. Fahrenkopf Jr.

Opponents of taxpayer financing of congressional elections claim that it would give government too big of a role in election competition. In the following viewpoint, Frank J. Fahrenkopf Jr. argues against a bill sponsored by Senators Robert Byrd (D-WV) and David Boren (D-OK). The bill, which would make government money available to candidates for Congress, would give unfair advantage to incumbents, according to Fahrenkopf. He believes that taxpayer financing of campaigns will allow elected officials to be less accountable to their constituents and less willing to work within the political system. Fahrenkopf is the chairman of the Republican National Committee.

As you read, consider the following questions:

1. Why does Fahrenkopf believe public financing of election campaigns aids incumbents more than challengers?
2. How will public financing of campaigns weaken the two-party system, according to the author? Why does he see this as being harmful?
3. What recommendations does Fahrenkopf make for improving the system of campaign financing?

Frank J. Fahrenkopf Jr., "Is the System Really Sick?" Republican National Committee press release on July 2, 1987. Reprinted with permission.

Those members of Congress arguing for massive changes in our campaign financing system would be wise to heed the Hippocratic Oath, which prohibits physicians from using "cures" that are more harmful than the disease. Congressional prescriptions for the ills of our campaign financing process, like the Boren-Byrd "public-financing" bill, are much more dangerous than the alleged disease.

Our present system of funding congressional elections *is* public-financing. The public voluntarily decides who will receive its financial support. What Senators Byrd and Boren are now proposing is to force the taxpayers to finance *their* campaigns.

Incumbents Protected

This kind of taxpayer-financing would protect incumbents from the public. There is already less and less need for legislators to talk to their constituents, as individuals and as groups. As former Senator Eugene McCarthy said in testimony against public-financing before a Senate Committee: "The isolation of political leaders from influences of individuals and groups sounds like, and is, totalitarianism."

Taxpayer-financing, like so many other well-intentioned government spending programs, also involves the government precisely in an arena it should venture into only with great trepidation—regulating the political debate. It is appropriate that government agencies and officials be responsible for the balloting, counting, and certifying of election results, with participant supervision. The proponents of taxpayer-financing would change this traditional neutral role and turn the government, in a sense, into a monolithic political committee.

Our doctors of reform also argue that all candidates would get equal funding, and that equal funding is equal treatment. But what they would really give us would be "The Congressional Incumbent Protection Act of 1987."

Incumbents already have the advantages of free media coverage, millions of dollars of sophisticated franked mailings which often look more like political advertising than informational newsletters, and official travel funds. Challengers have to spend more time and more money to have anything approximating equal visibility and political impact in their campaigns. "Equal treatment" would move members of Congress that much closer to becoming life peers. America does not need a House of Lords.

Two-Party System Damaged

Any taxpayer-financing system would also inevitably erode our two-party system, supplanting one of the principal functions of political parties—providing political and financial support to party candidates. Additionally, it would seriously endanger the traditional two-party political structure of the United States, balkanizing our political process by providing a taxpayer-financed incentive for creating splinter political campaigns.

For any taxpayer-financing system to be Constitutional, it would have to permit reasonable and attainable access to federal financing by third-party and independent congressional candidates. It would encourage candidates to run for office to push their particular issue or cause without any actual intent to hold office. Federal funding in 1980 and 1984 of Lyndon LaRouche's "campaigns" for president is a prime example of this aberration of the public-financing system.

New Forms of Bias

Public financing might eliminate whatever reinforcement contributions now give to lobbying, while substituting for the needed money that now comes from interested contributors. There are two problems with this approach. First, . . . eliminating direct contributions would not and could not eliminate the electoral role of interest groups. It would only introduce new forms of bias into the system. Second, even if the idea were good in theory, it would stand little chance of being adopted. Members of Congress are not likely ever to give their opponents enough money, solely from public funds, to permit serious challenges in expensive districts. Incumbents cannot be expected to think first about the system's need for electoral insecurity as they design the rules for their own reelection campaigns.

Michael Malbin, *Money and Politics in the United States,* 1984.

Our present system provides an incentive for political parties to incorporate single interest groups, third parties, and other legitimate expressions on social and political issues. The two major parties are a mechanism for compromise and fusion.

Taxpayer-financing would turn these incentives on their head. There would be a financial advantage in fragmenting our political system. Once a movement reached the crucial threshold of the public coffers, it would be against its personal/financial interests to work within the existing political framework.

Strengthen Political Parties

If Congress believes it must apply some treatment, two areas should be examined: 1) strengthening political parties, and 2) strengthening the disclosure requirements of our present law.

The Federal Election Campaign Act should be amended to permit parties to play a larger role in the financing of their candidates' campaigns. The only purpose recognized by the Supreme Court for limiting contributions to, or expenditures for, candidates is corruption or the appearance of corruption (corruption being the impairment of integrity or the exercise of improper or undue influence).

The notion of party support corrupting candidates runs counter to virtually every theory of a political party's function in the United States. Simply stated, there is no reason to restrict the support that political candidates may receive from their party organizations. The present law permits the United Auto Workers or the National Conservative Political Action Committee to make unlimited independent expenditures on behalf of any candidate for federal office, but does not permit the Republican National Committee or the Democratic National Committee the same treatment. There is no rationale for this discrimination. The Boren-Byrd bill would further reduce party support of its federal candidates.

The often-expressed concern about the level of financial support candidates receive from PACs can be addressed by increasing the amount of party funding available for campaigns.

Disclosing "Soft Dollars"

In the area of disclosure, our present law works admirably, except in one particular area—"soft dollars" raised by national political party committees for campaign activities. "Soft dollars" are funds raised outside the limitations and restrictions of the Federal Election Campaign Act. The Republican National Committee *alone* voluntarily discloses this information, but the American electorate has the right to know the names of the financial supporters of *both* national political parties.

Money Not the Dominant Issue

More than fifty years ago Will Rogers observed, "Politics has got so expensive that it takes lots of money to even get beat with." Campaign financing is not a new issue. The financing of campaigns is important, but our discussions of this issue should not obscure the fact that party, candidates, and issues are still the dominant factors in deciding election results—not money.

Recognizing Deceptive Arguments

People who feel strongly about an issue use many techniques to persuade others to agree with them. Some of these techniques appeal to the intellect, some to the emotions. Many of them distract the reader or listener from the real issues.

Below are listed a few common examples of argumentation tactics. Most of them can be used either to advance an argument in an honest, reasonable way or to deceive or distract from the real issues. It is important for a critical reader to recognize these tactics in order to rationally evaluate an author's ideas.

a. *scare tactics*—the threat that if you don't do or don't believe this, something terrible will happen

b. *strawperson*—distorting or exaggerating an opponent's ideas to make one's own seem stronger

c. *personal attack*—criticizing an opponent *personally* instead of rationally debating his or her ideas

d. *slanters*—to persuade through inflammatory and exaggerated language instead of reason

e. *generalizations*—using statistics or facts to generalize about a population, place, or thing

f. *categorical statements*—stating something in a way implying that there can be no argument

g. *deductive reasoning*—claiming that since a and b are true, c is also true, although there may not be a connection between a and c

The following activity will allow you to sharpen your skills in recognizing deceptive reasoning. Some of the statements below are taken from the viewpoints in this chapter. *Beside each one, mark the letter of the type of deceptive appeal being used. More than one type of tactic may be applicable. If you believe the statement is not any of the listed appeals, write N.*

1. If we do not change the way campaigns are financed, our system of government will cease to be democratic.

2. Senators supporting public financing of campaigns merely want taxpayers to pay for their reelection.

3. The misguided attempts to change campaign financing are the work of the busybodies at Common Cause.

4. All elected officials ever think about is raising money.

5. Only the wealthy and the corporations benefit from the influence of PACs.

6. Watergate revealed that our government is for sale to the biggest contributor.

7. There is no good reason for restricting the amount of funds parties can give their their candidates.

8. Campaign finance "reform" is a respectable sounding idea that's really a fraud.

9. If we allow tax money to be used to finance election campaigns, we will be turning Congress into an entrenched aristocracy, a new House of Lords.

10. If PACs were promoting pornography instead of political views, liberals would be supporting PACs.

11. Campaign contributions are just modern, cleaned-up versions of the old-fashioned, under-the-table bribe.

12. The fact is that money is everything these days.

13. A candidate's ability to raise funds is a clear indication of his appeal to the voters.

14. When the majority of PAC money came from unions, we didn't hear any propaganda from the self-righteous liberal lobbies about how terrible PACs are.

Periodical Bibliography

The following articles have been selected to supplement the diverse views presented in this chapter.

Herbert E. Alexander	"Election Reform Is No Sure Bet," *Los Angeles Times,* January 8, 1987.
The Congressional Digest	"Limiting Political Action Committees," February 1987.
Amy Dockser	"Nice PAC You've Got Here . . . A Pity If Anything Should Happen to It," *The Washington Monthly,* January 1987.
Robert F. Drinan	"The 100th Congress: Who Will Elect It?" *America,* October 18, 1986.
Gregg Easterbrook	"The Business of Politics," *The Atlantic Monthly,* October 1986.
Thomas B. Edsall	"Party Politics: Money Changes Everything," *Harper's Magazine,* December 1986.
Meg Greenfield	"The Political Debt Bomb," *Newsweek,* April 6, 1987.
Brooks Jackson	"People Power for Political Parties," *The Wall Street Journal,* December 4, 1986.
Robert Kuttner	"Fat and Sassy," *The New Republic,* February 23, 1987.
The Nation	"UnPAC," April 11, 1987.
Andy Plattner	"The High Cost of Holding—and Keeping—Public Office," *U.S. News & World Report,* June 22, 1987.
Larry Sabato	"PAC's, Parties and Presidents," *Society,* May/June 1985.

3 CHAPTER

What Role Should the Media Play in US Elections?

AMERICA'S
ELECTIONS

Chapter Preface

The national news media are often accused of trivializing the election process. Critics point to the media's endless coverage of insignificant campaign developments and of the results of public opinion polls showing which candidate is in the lead. The media, these critics claim, treat elections as if they were horse races, and ignore both discussion of the issues and debate over which candidate is most capable. The media are also criticized for probing into the personal lives of candidates. Some argue that they do this more to get a sensational story than to give the public useful knowledge about potential leaders.

Defenders of the news media argue that they merely cover campaigns the way candidates run them. Campaigns are portrayed as races because they *are* races with winners and losers, and because the public has an interest in who is ahead. As for the issue of candidate privacy, some reporters argue that candidates typically present the positive sides of their private and family lives in an attempt to gain voter admiration and support. If candidates are going to use their families and their moral character as a sales pitch for votes, then reporters should scrutinize whether the candidates are being honest with the public. If the media do not carry out this watchdog role, say these supporters, they are not performing their duty to the voters.

Do the media shape both the campaigns and the election outcome? Or do the media merely provide a mirror to campaigns, magnifying the hucksterism that has always been a part of America's elections? The viewpoints in this chapter debate this issue.

"We don't need to be told again and again who will win the political 'superbowl.' ... *Concentrate on the issues and let the American people do the rest."*

The Media Should Focus on Issues

Keith Blume

Critics of the news media complain the election coverage focuses too much on which candidate is leading in the race. In the following viewpoint, Keith Blume, using television coverage as an example, argues that the media must shift their coverage away from who's leading in the polls. Instead, election coverage should take the form of in-depth reports on the issues and more substantive portrayals of the candidates. Blume writes and produces television programs on world hunger and the nuclear arms race.

As you read, consider the following questions:

1. Why is the author critical of the labels that the media use to describe candidates?
2. According to Blume, in what ways were the media's coverage of issues like the budget deficit and defense spending inadequate? How does he think such issues should be covered?
3. What changes would Blume make to improve media election coverage?

Keith Blume, *The Presidential Election Show.* South Hadley, MA: Bergin & Garvey Publishers, 1985. Reprinted by permission.

The Presidential Election Show in 1984 was a flop by any standard of journalistic integrity. It was in fact a "show" and hardly journalism at all. It was almost certainly a negative influence in terms of participatory democracy, which neither the nation nor the planet can afford at this juncture in history. These comments apply particularly to CBS, ABC, NBC, and CNN. . . . "The MacNeil/Lehrer NewsHour" was in a league apart, far superior in some ways, but also sharing some of the defects of the commercial network programs. And it must also be stated plainly that to a significant degree, the print media demonstrated many of the same failings of television. But television is where the real action is in terms of audience, and by definition of the characteristics of the medium, its impact is unique. The following summation of the failures of television coverage of the presidential campaign illustrate a format and approach that must be radically altered if television is to rescue its honor and its right to apply the term "journalism" to its news programming.

Media Shallowness

Theodore White, in his book *America in Search of Itself*, noted that the weekend before election day in 1980 was the one-year anniversary of the Iranian hostage crisis, and all the networks aired special reports reminding the electorate of the Americans still held captive by the Iranians. Throughout the weekend, the constant images of impotence and humiliation flooded America's TV screens. What had been a close race turned to a rout, the polls showing major movement toward Reagan in the forty-eight hours before the polls opened. By running its nightly update on "America Held Hostage" (the forerunner of "Nightline"), ABC was perhaps the single greatest influence in the defeat of Jimmy Carter. The operative words here are *image* and *repetition*. By creating an image and repeating it over and over again, television has an immeasurable impact. The Iranian hostage crisis was certainly not the single most important issue before this country every day for over a year, but the image created by television made it seem so, which, politically, made it so. ABC News didn't care whether or not it was good journalism, because it was a good "show," bringing good ratings and good money. . . .

In March, 1985, [Ted] Koppel and "Nightline" gave the consummate demonstration of what broadcast journalism *could* accomplish with the extraordinary programs from South Africa. With Koppel's talents unleashed on the same story for an entire week, a truly informative process took place. But why was this approach never utilized to cover issues during the presidential campaign? And how often did "Nightline" cover campaign-related stories? Wouldn't one expect at least half of the reports between Labor Day and election day to do so? Divide by four and you will be closer. And when there were election-related stories, they seldom concentrated in depth on issues. This was also true of the weekly CBS election report with Dan Rather, which was not much more than a weekly recap of the evening news highlights. The greatest contribution by CBS's "60 Minutes" to democracy during the campaign (September 16, 1984) was by Andy Rooney in one of his supposedly folksy, wise, humorous comments. He informed us "that the presidential election is too long. If it was a television show it would be canceled after four weeks." He neglected to observe that it was a television show, a very bad one precisely because of the shallowness of the video-noninformation pushers such as himself. In a stunning display of his intellectual depth and commitment to democracy, he told us that everyone knew how the vote would turn out, so we should get it over with. NBC didn't even bother with special programming, which was just as well, all things considered. . . .

STARVATION DIET

© Rosen/Rothco.

Every night on the nightly news programs, image and repetition was the operative approach. Ronald Reagan was the Great Communicator and his reelection was inevitable. Walter Mondale was "boring" and his challenge was impossible. To think that the constant repetition of these images does not have an enormous impact on the electorate would be to have one's head in the sand. This cannot be confirmed by a poll, of course. How can one ask the conscious mind how the unconscious mind had been affected by such a bombardment? The first thing TV news must do is examine its descriptive language, its assumptions, its preoccupation with strategy and polls. Was Ronald Reagan such a great communicator during the debates, or anytime without a prepared script and proper staging? Was Walter Mondale that bad on TV, or not bad at all when the commentators and evening news editors got out of the way, as during the first debate? How many times during the year was the volatility of the polls demonstrated? So why keep talking about them, analyzing them, worshiping them, reinforcing them, and so on? After the first debate, Reagan's own polls showed Mondale picking up ten points in a week, a momentum, if continued, that would have resulted in a Mondale landslide! What caused this and the other wild swings after the Democratic Convention and after the second debate? As we have seen, TV images had much to do with it in all cases. It is a vicious circle. It is impossible to decipher precisely the entanglements of this TV-image, repetitious, poll-taking, poll-reporting monster that feeds on itself. But it is easy to recommend what to do with this entire intellectually empty approach: Throw it into the junkyard of video political history. We don't need the media labels pinned on the candidates for us, defining for us who they are. We don't need to be told again and again who will win the political "superbowl," or the statistics that prove by reinforcing until fact. Concentrate on the issues and let the American people do the rest. . . .

Missing the Issues

Consider just a few of the issues that were either covered so briefly as to be meaningless or missed entirely by TV "journalism."

After the first presidential debate, on CNN's "Crossfire," Jody Powell observed that Reagan was being disingenuous about taxes and Mondale disingenuous about Social Security and Medicare, in both cases because the deficit had become a crisis that could leave no one's sacred cows untouched. The one thing that must be said for Mondale is that, whereas his political use of Social Security resulted in Reagan following suit, Reagan's political use of the tax issue did not result in Mondale's abandoning his politically "losing" position [in favor of raising taxes]. On the other hand, it must also be said that Mondale, far behind in the polls, was playing political poker, gambling that the American people would face reality and see him as a "leader" for taking a "courageous" and honest stand. But the television coverage of these issues was almost always focused on the political rather than the policy implications, contributing to the freezing of responses on the issues by the campaigns in outworn political modes, instead of contributing to a focus on the need for rethinking positions in the face of new realities.

97

Responsible issue-oriented news coverage requires including historical background as a prelude to discussing present policy options. For example, where during the campaign did we see a lengthy and thorough report on the history of Social Security? How many Americans know that the massive program it has become bears little resemblance to the concept originally proposed by Franklin Roosevelt? How many Americans know that from 1960 to 1984 the percentage of gross national product spent on Social Security and Medicare jumped from 2.3 percent to 6.6 percent? And where during the campaign did we see a detailed examination of the economic realities and options for Social Security and Medicare over the next several decades, and how these factors influence present potential policy decisions? All of this is to say nothing of the larger issue of the crisis of government spending in general. It was easy politically for Mondale to challenge Reagan on never cutting these programs, but how realistically would he have dealt with the black-hole economics involved?

Taking the Easy Route

Candidates are only human, after all: most will take the easy route if you let them, do the parades and the baby-kissing, eat the pizzas and dance the polkas. That's a lot less wearing than proving to us their capacity to unite and lead the American people. So the press has to force campaigns and candidates out of the style and the show-biz glitter and into the substance.

Herb Schmertz, *Conservative Chronicle*, November 4, 1987.

Consider another aspect of this crisis: defense spending. Reagan periodically attacked Mondale as being weak on defense, but the fact was, both candidates favored increasing the defense budget substantially, although Reagan wanted a rate of increase approximately twice the size of Mondale's. The defense budget had approximately doubled in four years, the fastest rate of growth in peacetime by far in American history. Where did we see an in-depth analysis of the impact of defense spending in terms of specific weapons systems, military strategy, economic impact on jobs and the deficit, particularly since the accelerated Reagan buildup began in 1981? . . . These were the kind of difficult and crucial issues that should have been discussed and debated before the American electorate, with the media leading the way in the examination process. . . .

These examples are only a few among many. It is impossible, and indeed useless, to discuss issues without expressing a viewpoint. But the primary point here is not the author's perspective on these issues, but the lack of TV news coverage of the issues themselves. It is the job of responsible journalism to present both point and counterpoint as fairly as possible. But first must come the commitment to really examine at length the major policy questions of our time. As has been previously stated, only "The MacNeil/Lehrer NewsHour" approaches such subjects with any depth. To ascend from the abyss to the plane the medium is capable of, and the American electorate in need of, the commercial networks and MacNeil/Lehrer as well must first eliminate the horse-race and image-making approaches already described here. Then the commercial networks must take the obvious step of extending their news programs to one hour and adopting a format similar to that of MacNeil/Lehrer, mixing in-depth visual and voice-over reports with pertinent interviews, with greater emphasis on "reporting" on the issues, laying out the basic facts and different sides of policy arguments. Interviews are excellent supplements, but by their nature cannot impart information with the same effectiveness as a good report. Even if the commercial newscasts remain at their present length, they should at least devote the majority of time to the campaign, incorporating the above recommendations. During a presidential campaign, there should be additional special programming, taking the same approach just described, preferably every evening. On the commercial networks, it is conceivable that public financing in terms of "buying time" could play a role, in effect creating "islands" of public television on the commercial networks during the campaign. It is even theoretically possible for the Federal Communications Commission or the Congress to mandate the public use of air time in this regard. But the implementation of the journalistic reforms recommended here will likely ultimately occur only if the networks opt for integrity over dollars, at least for a few months every four years. Enlightened self-interest could potentially lead to a marriage of integrity and profit in broadcast journalism. . . . The historical record does not make one overly optimistic, but I believe in the possibility of salvation. . . .

Kick the Junk Habit

Real journalistic integrity on the part of television demands continuing programming that will explore honestly and in depth the public-policy questions of our time as the essential definition of "news." This cannot happen just during a presidential election campaign, but must be an ongoing process. Of course it may require, at first, dragging some viewers kicking and screaming to the "classroom." That is the price of addicting people to junk. And the networks will have to start by kicking the habit themselves.

"The public's interest in who is winning and who is lagging is inevitable and legitimate."

The Media Should Focus on Who Is Winning

David S. Broder

In the following viewpoint, David Broder contends that the public is interested in who is ahead and who is behind in an election campaign. Using newspaper coverage as an example, Broder contends that an important part of the media's job is to determine and report the public's mood and its perception of the candidates. Broder is a political reporter and syndicated columnist with *The Washington Post.*

As you read, consider the following questions:

1. According to Broder, who is responsible for the amount of emphasis on issues during a campaign? Do you agree or disagree? Why?
2. Why does the author believe reporting on which candidate is ahead and which is behind is a worthwhile task?
3. What suggestions does Broder make to improve campaign coverage?

David S. Broder, *Behind the Front Page.* Copyright © 1987 by David S. Broder. Reprinted by permission of SIMON & SCHUSTER, Inc.

Every day, the national political reporters are competing with each other. Within the club, we know which reporters are doing well and which ones aren't. And nothing so influences those collective opinions as each individual's skill or lack of skill to gauge the course of the campaign—knowing who is up and who is down.

A "Horse Race"

Our critics love to complain about our tendency to reduce the process of choosing the President to the dimensions of a horse race, with terms like front-runner and long shot. "Horse-race journalism," the critics say, emphasizes strategy and tactics and ignores issues, substance, and serious consideration of candidates' qualifications. . . .

James M. Perry of the *Wall Street Journal* was asked by the now-defunct journalism review *MORE*, in 1974, "Why do we do it?" The answers, he said, were all bad: "Tradition. Habit. Laziness. Because, sometimes, our editors want us to do it. Because we see politics as a kind of a game, a race between various performers, and we're the time-keepers. Because it's easy and because, maybe, it's fun."

I think horse-race journalism is all of that. But it is also a genuine and legitimate response to the curiosity about "who's going to win this thing?" It is a reasonable question to try to answer—if we have the skill to do it. If the mission is legitimate, as I believe, two questions still must concern political reporters: Can we judge the race well enough to make the effort worth attempting? And can we do that without losing sight of other aspects of the coverage—especially the issues? . . .

The Prediction Game

Since I came to [*The Washington Post*] in 1966, we have put together a state-by-state rundown of the races on the Sunday before the biennial general election. Our politicially hip readers use this twin-page summary as a checklist for the Tuesday night returns. But more than that, they can use all the information we have assembled to try to outguess the experts.

I recognize, as do the editors of the *Post*, the game quality of that preelection piece, and we go at it competitively. For the last week of the campaign, I pump every possible source for the latest information and judgment, drawing on other *Post* reporters, campaign consultants, and media advisers. After we add this mass of information to our own and others' latest polling and up-to-the-minute checks with political reporters in the fifty states, the time comes for judgment—for gut feelings.

From Thursday night until noon Saturday, Maralee Schwartz, our political researcher, and I sit down and call somewhere between 100 and 150 races. We are tough with ourselves. The easy way out—but not as much fun—is to hedge everything doubtful by calling it TCTC, Too Close To Call. Some races really must be put in that category. But if there is any discernible lean, even the slightest, we lean it that way—and take our chances.

For most elections in the late 1960s and the 1970s, the political researcher and I were right on 80 to 90 percent of the calls. (We could boost the percentage cheaply by calling all 435 House races, but we limit the House calls to the fifty or sixty districts with serious races.)

In 1980, when I sat down to write the Sunday preelection survey, two things stood out. The top of the story said, "Ronald Reagan has the pieces in place and the machinery to deliver a Republican presidential victory on Tuesday." Further down, it added, "Equally evident are the possible benefits to the GOP if the Reagan boom that was rolling from Wednesday through Friday should extend to Election Day. The reports to the *Post* indicated brightening Republican prospects in Tuesday's Senate races. There are 10 states where Republicans have a good to excellent chance to take over Democratic seats and only three where they risk losses." Republicans actually made a net gain of twelve seats.

Not Much News Value in Issues

Because the news is what is different about events of the past 24 hours, the newsworthiness of what a candidate says about public policies is limited. To be specific, once a candidate makes known his position on an issue, further statements concerning that issue decline in news value. . . . There are not enough major issues for the candidates to keep questions of policy at the top of the news for a full year. Thus the principal effect of a longer campaign is to spread a somewhat fixed amount of substance over a greater period of time.

Thomas Patterson, quoted in *Behind the Front Page,* 1987.

The story felt right to me (and one should not disguise the importance of gut instinct on that kind of question), in part because that is how the campaign had looked when it was just beginning. Immediately after Labor Day, I had gone back to the precincts, trying to test whether the appeal of Reagan to blue-collar voters that we often had seen in the primaries would show again in the general election. In the blue-collar neighborhoods of two states that would be crucial in a close election, Michigan and Texas, I found that, with inflation raging and Carter seemingly unable to deal with the Iranian hostage situation, a massive shift was in the making. Over and over I heard, "Let's try the other guy. It couldn't be worse."

Now, in the final week of the campaign, with both the economy and the hostages in the headlines, I did not doubt that Reagan would win. But Barry Sussman's scientific polling that week showed a very different picture. He and Robert Kaiser wrote that "just two days before the 1980 election, American voters remain narrowly divided in their choice for President and unusually volatile." Unable to decide between Sussman's too-close-to-call or Broder's Republican-win story, the *Post's* editors bravely put both stories on page one, in a display of journalistic schizophrenia that must have puzzled a good many of our readers that Sunday morning.

Why Bother?

In 1984 we faced no such problem, because both reporting and polling pointed toward the overwhelming Reagan victory. But in any year the serious question is: Why bother? My answer is that readers' curiosity about who is winning is real and we should try to satisfy it.

And I am not convinced that horse-race journalism blinds us— or the voters—to the importance of issues in the election. It is an old charge, one often made by in-house critics of the press. In *The Real Campaign*, [Jeff] Greenfield faulted "the media's fascination with itself as a political force and . . . its fundamental view that politics is more image than substance; that ideas, policies, positions, and intentions are simply the wrappings in which a power struggle takes place." Greenfield's comments were echoed by many others, including Haynes Johnson. But do we "neglect" the issues?

Elections are contests between individuals, not between philosophies. Voters choose between Candidate A and Candidate B, not between liberalism and conservatism, high or low taxes, permissive or restrictive abortion policies. Voters know that history is replete with examples of Presidents who did exactly the opposite of what they had pledged to do in the campaign. Franklin Roosevelt campaigned for a balanced budget and created the welfare state. Lyndon Johnson campaigned against intervention in Vietnam and intervened. Jimmy Carter campaigned for a simplification and decentralization of government and added two new cabinet departments. Ronald Reagan campaigned for fiscal austerity and ran up record deficits.

Still, voters care about issues as they affect their own lives. Inflation, recession, the threat of war or higher taxes or toxic wastes are not abstractions but real concerns to people. Voters use issues to weigh the capabilities of the candidates and to refine their own feelings about the candidates' personalities and character. But the presidency is ultimately a test of character as much or more than a test of policy and management. And we are not mistaken if we focus primarily on the people who are candidates.

103

In some campaigns issues are of no real importance. In 1976, both Carter and Ford went to the public with one simple proposition: "I am the sort of person you can trust with the power of the presidency." Two years after Watergate, it was not surprising that the trust question dwarfed all other issues. Any reporter who tried to cast Ford and Carter—both essentially men of the middle—as having sharply contrasting philosophies and programs would have distorted reality.

Elections Are Contests

The political jargon is awash in the clichés of sports: winning or losing the game, campaign teams and their managers, public-opinion polls handicapping the horse race, candidates (often called "horses") jockeying for position and so on. The similarities between politics and sports are striking and obvious.

An election is, first of all, a contest among competitors striving for the same prize. If you work for one of them you are said to be, as in boxing, in his corner. In a debate, one candidate may score a knockout, or the event may be judged a draw. A single day on which several presidential primaries are held was originally called—what else?—Super Bowl Tuesday, now shortened to Super Tuesday. The language of the playing field or arena is too apropos to politics, and too integral, to be avoided.

Jack Germond and Jules Witcover, *Wake Us When It's Over*, 1985.

Nonetheless, James McCartney, a veteran correspondent in the Knight-Ridder chain's Washington bureau, said the prevalence of what he called "junk news" was not entirely the candidates' fault. "The media simply never took issues seriously on their own terms," he wrote after the 1976 election in the *Columbia Journalism Review*. "The press in all of its branches—written and electronic—often would fail to report speeches on serious issues at all, or if it did, it would often fail to present them straight: issues, if mentioned at all, would be buried in stories constructed around other subjects—strategy and tactics, evaluations of candidates' momentum, and all of the other kinds of political small talk that arise in any campaign."

Such criticisms had an effect on the 1980 campaign coverage, but the real difference was the candidates' willingness to focus on the issues. Carter was forced, willy-nilly, to defend his record in office. Reagan had always been an issue advocate, almost an ideologue as those things are reckoned in American politics, and he talked regularly, not just about Carter's failings, but about the basic changes he would make: a major, across-the-board tax cut; a sharp slowdown in the growth of domestic programs; a significant shift of resources from the domestic budget to expanded military defense. . . .

As always, we covered the campaign as the candidates conducted it. Reporters can complain that a President is ducking press conferences and not talking substantively about issues, but there is no way to do stories about speeches that are not given, press conferences that are not held.

"Inside Baseball"

The outcome of the 1984 election was probably sealed well in advance, when Reagan escaped an assassin's bullet in 1981, when he showed his mastery of Congress in that summer's tax and budget fights, when he cut short his mistaken military intervention in Lebanon, and when the economy soared from recession in 1983 without reigniting inflation.

In such a climate, we often succumbed to the temptation to look past the coming election and examine whether this was just a personal triumph for Reagan or the second stage in a rolling realignment that might give the Republican Party long-term ascendancy in politics. It was an intriguing question—but essentially one that interested the insiders in the clique more than the broad public. As Milton Coleman of the *Post* and Jim Lehrer of PBS's "MacNeil/Lehrer NewsHour" told an American University forum, there was too much of "our own preoccupation with inside baseball" in the 1984 campaign coverage.

Certainly, 1984 was not a year in which either the politicians or the press distinguished themselves. It left many people—including most of my colleagues and myself—wondering if we had done all that we might to make the election the dialogue about the country's future which it ideally should have been.

Improving Campaign Coverage

There are two or three things we might do to improve campaign coverage, particularly during the critical final phase. We in the newspapers need to recognize, explicitly, the different needs of different parts of our audience. Without interrupting the continuity of coverage, around September we need to say, "Okay, for those of you who are just tuning in on the fact that there's an election coming, here is what you need to know about the people running." We could clear the ads from a couple pages and lay out what we think we know about the backgrounds, careers, and views of the candidates.

We have to realize, however, that not every reader who needs that kind of summary will take the time or trouble to read it. One of the inherent weaknesses of journalism is that we cannot reach out, grab the reader by the shoulders, shake him, and command, "Read this. It's important. It tells you what you need to know."

Television, with its "depth" pieces running only five minutes, has an even tougher time being comprehensive and comprehensible. It is always chancy how much closely compacted information, delivered through a picture medium, will remain in a viewer's mind. Perhaps somewhere in our multilayered communication system of radio, television, newspapers, news magazines, monthlies, and even campaign books the voter will find as much information as he really craves—and is ready to absorb. . . .

There are other things the press and television can do to deepen the discussion of issues, such as running a substantial chunk of a candidate's speech or a statement dealing substantively with policy and comparing his views with those of his opponent. Lyn Nofziger, Reagan's longtime adviser and former press secretary, complained at an American University forum following the 1984 campaign that we tend to forget this basic obligation, particularly late in the campaign. The *New York Times* periodically runs a long excerpt from the candidate's basic speech, the one he repeats substantially unchanged from rally to rally. It's an idea I would not be ashamed to see the *Post* imitate.

But candidates now tailor their comments for the short soundbites usable on the nightly television news shows. The pattern of their discourse can be changed by changing or broadening the format. If, during the campaign season, the networks made available a regular ten-minute or fifteen-minute prime-time block for talks by the candidates, it would be an offer no candidate could refuse. The networks ought to specify the topic for the week and retain control of the format. If the candidates knew, for example, that they had ten minutes to outline their views on unemployment in the basic industries, they would very quickly find something substantive to say on the subject. You can convey a great deal in ten minutes—or make it evident that you really have no ideas to offer. The system has worked well in Great Britain and for party spokesmen on public television's "MacNeil/Lehrer NewsHour." Campaign managers also complain that they are forced to use thirty-second ads because the networks and stations are reluctant to disrupt their regular programming to sell them time for five-minute commercials.

A Legitimate Interest

So we in the media could make changes to give better structure and definition to the policy side of the campaign. But I would not concede that this is an argument against horse-race coverage. I end, as I began, with the view that the public's interest in who is winning and who is lagging is inevitable and legitimate and human.

"Far from being overly aggressive about invading people's privacy, American journalism is paralyzed by gentility."

The Media Should Report on Candidates' Private Lives

Michael Kinsley

In May 1987 Democratic presidential candidate Gary Hart withdrew from the presidential race after the news media reported that he had apparently spent the night with a young model while his wife was out of town. These revelations caused a heated discussion among journalists. How much should they tell about the private lives of candidates for office? In the following viewpoint, Michael Kinsley contends that candidates bring this kind of scrutiny upon themselves. Kinsley, the editor of *The New Republic*, argues that the media should report what they know, and let the voters decide whether what is revealed is important or not.

As you read, consider the following questions:

1. Why, according to Kinsley, are candidates themselves to blame for the media's probing into their lives?
2. Why does the author think that those journalists who hold back information about the private affairs of candidates are elitist?

Michael Kinsley, "On the Zipper Beat," *The New Republic*, May 25, 1987. Reprinted by permission of THE NEW REPUBLIC, © 1987, The New Republic, Inc.

The fuss over Gary Hart's alleged dirty weekend is giving everybody a chance to quote from Macauley: "We know of no spectacle so ridiculous as the British public in one of its periodic fits of morality." Well, I know of one spectacle more ridiculous: the American press in one of its periodic fits of self-flagellation.

Paralyzed by Gentility

Far from being overly aggressive about invading people's privacy, American journalism is paralyzed by gentility in comparison to newspapers in Britain and elsewhere. Nobody forced Gary Hart to run for president, and nobody forced him to spend a weekend cavorting, carnally or otherwise, with another middle-aged married man and a couple of chicks half their age. This kind of behavior seems to be a congenital disease of politicians. The same juices that drive them to run for office drive many to horse around and may drive some to express themselves in other ways, like starting wars. This needs watching. They don't call it power lust for nothing.

Anything that keeps a politician humble and slightly unnerved is healthy for democracy. So is the regular reminder to the electorate of how ridiculous politicians can be. The pageant of human folly is valuable for its own sake, too. If politicians are going to run our lives, the least we can expect in return is to get some entertainment value out of them.

Candidates Invite Scrutiny

Journalists, though, are also somewhat full of ourselves. We need a more ennobling rationale for sitting all night in a car outside someone else's Capitol Hill town house. In Hart's case, there is the so-called "character issue." Many journalists also cling with relief to the fact that Hart, out of some weird self-destructive impulse, actually invited the press to try and catch him womanizing. "Follow me around, I don't care," he told the *New York Times.* "I'm serious. If anybody wants to put a tail on me, go ahead. They'd be very bored."

But Hart has invited such scrutiny in a larger sense, too, and so has almost every other politician in America. Hart says he wants to talk about the issues, his new ideas, and so on, not his personal life. But he has been talking about his personal life over and over again. He could have answered the inevitable questions about womanizing by saying. "The state of my marriage is nobody's business." Instead, he has painted a rather detailed picture of a marriage that went through some rocky times and emerged stronger than ever. He says he doesn't womanize. If that's not true, he's a liar, and lying is a legitimate issue by the hoitiest of toity standards.

No politician really keeps his private life private—only the parts of his private life he thinks the voters won't appreciate. If political candidates kept their wives and children and church volunteer activities out of the campaign, they'd be on firmer ground when insisting that their girlfriends or boyfriends or unsavory hobbies are irrelevant. What the press is protecting when it fails to report such things is not privacy. It's hypocrisy.

Let the Voters Decide

We are witnessing the breakdown, at long last, of an anti-democratic conspiracy among the Washington elite of journalists and politicians. The conspiracy was intended to keep information from the mass of voters that these benighted troglodytes couldn't be trusted with. The high-minded argument is that such matters are irrelevant to a person's fitness for office. The real motivation is fear that many citizens will disagree.

Not Digging Deep Enough

We have to say we are no longer bound by unwritten rules or "gentlemen's agreements" that deny to our readers information they need to make judgments as citizens. . . .

The modern presidency shows that it is the unexplored questions of policy, reputation, record and, yes, character that come back to haunt us. The indictment of American journalism is not that we go too far, but that we too often don't dig deep enough.

David S. Broder, *Washington Post National Weekly Edition*, May 25, 1987.

So what would have happened if the voters had known about FDR's liaison with Eleanor's social secretary, Lucy Mercer? I don't know what would have happened. It doesn't matter. Either you believe in democracy, in which case you trust in or at least tolerate the result, or you don't. Even in a democracy, of course, there are good reasons for keeping some information secret. But concern about its effect in the voting booth is not a good reason.

Journalists are understandably suffering from a bit of vertigo as they peer down a novel trail, steep and winding, and wonder where it will lead. Is there no limit on what we should feel free, or even obligated, to publish about people's private lives? Of course there is. I propose a simple test. Is this something that you believe a significant fraction of your audience will find politically relevant? Not just interesting (we all love gossip): Will it affect how people vote? If so, go with it. Who are you to say it's none of their business.

Thoughtful observers (those inveterate party poopers) worry that relentless scrutiny of private foibles will drive good people out of public office, and leave us with gray automatons who have nothing to hide. I doubt that the flame of political ambition can be snuffed so easily. In any event, why do Washington sophisticates suppose that this is a danger that voters around the country can't also recognize and account for?

No Fit of Morality

It's possible that politicians and journalists underestimate the sophistication of their constituents and readers. Representative Gerry Studds gets regularly reelected in Massachusetts after having admitted a liaison with a male congressional page. In Nebraska—Nebraska!—Governor Bob Kerry's poll ratings shot up every time actress Debra Winger came for a weekend in the governor's mansion. Someday a presidential candidate will say to the voters: look, my marriage is a bust, I'm only human, I need a little relief from the pressures of public life. And the voters may turn out to understand this just as well as the elitists who want to keep such obvious truths from them.

The candidate won't be Gary Hart. Even before the town house episode, he had publicly locked himself into the conventions of rectitude. The fact that he did so and then apparently couldn't adhere to them—even for a few months—raises doubts about his judgment and self-control that must trouble even the most principled Dionysian.

Nevertheless, I sense no "fit of morality" erupting among the American public. If the new honesty in the press about politicians' canoodling leads to more honesty among politicians themselves, we might well find that the voters really don't care so much what elected officials do in private. Then we can go back to discussing the issues, as everybody hypocritically claims to want.

..

4

"Every normal person has something intimate to hide. In matters of private conscience, the right to be defended is the public's right not to know."

The Media Should Not Report on Candidates' Private Lives

Ross K. Baker and William Safire

Some journalists are disturbed by the increased coverage of the private lives of candidates for office. In Part I of the following viewpoint, Ross K. Baker claims that the media have needlessly abandoned a long-honored code of restraint in their coverage of candidates. In Part II, William Safire argues that politicians must take the lead in refusing to cooperate with the media's probing into their private lives. Otherwise, campaign coverage will degenerate into nothing but gossip and titillation. Baker is a political science professor at Rutgers University. Safire is a syndicated columnist for *The New York Times.*

As you read, consider the following questions:

1. According to Baker, why do the media no longer practice restraint in their coverage of candidates?
2. What advice does Safire give to candidates bombarded with personal questions by reporters? Why does he believe this is an effective approach?

Ross K. Baker, "The Watchdog Press Slips the Leash of Propriety," *Los Angeles Times,* May 7, 1987. Reprinted with the author's permission.
William Safire, "Stop Keyhole Journalism," *The New York Times,* May 11, 1987. Copyright © 1987 by The New York Times Company. Reprinted by permission.

I

The Rev. Martin Luther King Jr. was a womanizer who rationalized his behavior by noting that the leadership of the civil-rights movement put him under enormous emotional pressure. According to David J. Garrow's Pulitzer prize-winning biography, *Bearing the Cross,* King defended his sexual athleticism as "a form of tension reduction."

While King was subjected to merciless harassment for his sexual adventures by FBI Director J. Edgar Hoover, the newspapers never touched the subject. Nor did they inquire into the many sexual liaisons of Presidents John F. Kennedy and Lyndon B. Johnson. Dwight D. Eisenhower's war-time affair with Kay Summersby Morgan did not come to light until the publication of her memoirs 30 years after the fact. Most journalists of the day never knew about the most durable of all presidential affairs—that of President Franklin D. Roosevelt and Lucy Mercer Rutherford. Yet the Roosevelt affair produced a peculiar standoff at the time of the 1940 presidential election when word came to the Roosevelt campaign that the Republican nominee, Wendell L. Willkie, was romantically involved with a woman who was not his wife. Roosevelt's campaign managers feared that the President's own secret might be exposed if they raised the subject of his opponent's infidelity.

A Code of Discretion

Why did none of this information ever reach the public? The answer is found in the code of discretion that prevailed among journalists until very recently and that still causes some of them to be queasy about reporting the intimate details of the lives of public figures.

The code was a simple and straightforward one: If the private behavior of a public official was not criminal and did not adversely affect the conduct of that official's duties, it was no business of the press to report it.

The dutiful watchdog, however, has lately been transformed into a snarling attack dog—or at least a dyspeptic bloodhound—that can be found rooting around in everything from Henry Kissinger's trash can to Gary Hart's driveway.

The transformation of the press from the attentive guardians of public rectitude into an unrestrained pack of yapping terriers came about because of changes both in politics and in journalism. The turning point probably came in the 1970s as a consequence of the Watergate scandal and the manner in which it was exposed and the quick succession of sensational revelations of Sen. Frank Church's committee during its investigation of the CIA.

By this time, moreover, presidential politics had evolved into an exercise in marketing images on television—a development that challenged journalists to discover the real person lurking behind the mask fashioned by media advisers. Journalists were discovering the tools of aggressive investigative reporting about the same time that politicians were perfecting new techniques of presenting themselves to the public in the most flattering, even heroic, light. If politicians were going to parade around like white knights, the watchdog was going to need teeth sharp enough to pierce the suit of armor.

Reporters on a Rampage

Rather than resulting in a nice equilibrium in which journalistic enterprise and skepticism balanced off presidential image-making, many reporters allowed themselves to be gulled by the electronic facades of Presidents or presidential candidates and to write adoringly of them. But at the first sign that the image they had so lovingly nurtured might be concealing a less noble reality, the reporters would be seized by distemper and go on a rampage.

What is distressing is how little of this new aggressiveness is directed toward policies that are advocated by the candidates and how much of it is just sneering and leering.

Politicians, foolishly, invite such probing. Jimmy Carter, with his smirking sanctimony, virtually dared the press to pick a hole in his coat, and then gave it the tool to accomplish that with his "lust in the heart" statement. Hart, with his challenge to news organizations to assign reporters to "put a tail on me," was dan-

Mike Keefe. Reprinted with permission.

gling a hunk of red meat in front of a Doberman, and couldn't blame the dog for going after the toothsome morsel. Hart had been forthright with the press about the two separations from his wife, and made no profession of celibacy for that period. He was not trying to fob himself off as a plaster saint. There was no need for him to publicly model his chastity belt, especially if he were going to continue a pattern of behavior that suggested wickedness.

But the Hart scandal raises a larger question of just how much time serious journalists ought to spend at the keyhole on stories designed to cause the public to drool and slaver over politicians' peccadilloes. The presidency is a special case, to be sure, but the Constitution does not require chastity of those who would aspire to the office.

A Standard of Conduct

If "womanizing" is fair game for the press, what about a longtime liaison between a candidate and just one woman? And if all we know of a negative nature about a presidential candidate is that he occasionally sleeps with a woman other than his wife, does it become a disqualifying flaw? Calvin Coolidge was faithful to his wife, and Franklin Roosevelt was not. Can anyone argue that the man who adhered to the conventional morality was a better President? Would unmasking Martin Luther King as a womanizer and hypocrite have enriched us in any way?

Before journalists slip the leash of journalistic propriety and tear off to sniff out the private lives of public people, they might consider a simple but fair standard of conduct. If it's not impeachable, it's not reachable.

II

"Have you ever committed adultery?" was the stone some sin-free questioner lobbed at Gary Hart. His answer was a temperate "I do not have to answer that question." Mine would have been "Go to hell."

Neither the media nor the government has a right to expect an answer to such personal questions. We would all be better off if candidates for office were expected to take offense at such intrusions.

"Go to Hell"

Ah, but hadn't Mr. Hart's comings and goings caused a furor, which made fidelity an issue in his campaign? Certainly he foolishly ignored all the red flags, but we cannot fairly use a press furor as a self-generating excuse for overboard inquisitions. Media protestations to the contrary, future surveillance is not likely to be limited to candidates who provide "probable cause."

Suppose a candidate is accused of homosexuality, perhaps by a publicity seeker, or a rejected spouse or fired campaign aide,

114

or a person paid by the political opposition. Some magazine will find a high-minded reason for obliquely referring to the charge. At a news conference, a reporter eager to win an instant reputation for investigativism asks, "In the light of all these printed reports, have you ever had a homosexual experience?"

Advice to candidates: Do not respond. Even the most measured denial might trigger the headline "Straight From Candidate: 'I Am Not Gay.'" That would spread the notion that you are a homosexual. Instead, express your disgust at the reporter for demeaning his or her profession, and conclude with the phrase that will earn you respect among voters and serious journalists: Go to hell.

Let Candidates Decide

The press is at its most self-righteous in asserting its prerogatives to ask everything about anything. Its defense is that it asks personal questions of the candidates because of the public's right to know. That, however, begs the question: Who gave the press the right to decide what is the public's right to know? . . .

The candidates for our highest office are not just choirboys waiting for instructions from the holy airwaves on the tune they're supposed to hum. Candidates ought to decide what in their personal backgrounds is necessary for the public to know, put it out in their official campaign material and leave it at that. At the same time they should understand that if they are hiding something important it will eventually come out.

If the candidates are confident that they have leveled with the public, they should then be confident enough to tell the press to "get stuffed."

Robert G. Beckel, *Minneapolis Star Tribune*, November 24, 1987.

Suppose a female candidate takes a strong right-to-life stand. Under the New Rules of Bluenose Journalism, that would make legitimate this question: "Have you ever had an abortion?" or "Did your own daughter tell you why she was in the hospital on such and such a date?" The only answer both proper and politic: Go to hell.

If we do not turn the tables on the titillaters, we will load future news conferences with such significant policy questions as: "Sir, there are widespread reports of your impotence; when was the last time you and your wife had sexual relations?" "Madam, how do you deal with the persistant rumors that your national security adviser is a herpes victim?" "Have you or any member of your family ever taken illegal drugs?" "Some say that you once saw a psychiatrist—exactly what was your problem?"

Every normal person has something intimate to hide. In matters of private conscience, the right to be defended is the public's right not to know. Nobody should be forced to lie about what is nobody else's business, or to confess, as Jimmy Carter felt called upon to do, to even such a common sin as lust in our hearts.

Recipients of salacious tips should examine the motive of the tipster and beware of being manipulated in an entrapment scheme.

Peccadilloes with a partner who shares a bed with a Russian agent (Profumo) or a Mafia don (Kennedy), or by a head of state arriving at a summit conference with a harem of stewardesses (Brezhnev) bear on national security and deserve to be reported. But the old press protectiveness need not be replaced by a new nakedness; secret surveillance of politicians by reporters is in the same sleazy category as secret wiretapping of reporters by politicians.

Limits of Privacy

Privacy for candidates should stop where wealth and health begin. People who want to assume the public trust should be willing to give up their privacy on matters of money and illness. Tell us your holdings and show us your tax returns; that avoids conflict of interest and makes it much easier to prevent dishonesty. And level with us in detail on medical prognoses on matters that may affect your performance in office.

But no public figure, not even a porno star, should have to bare his or her soul or take polygraph tests on personal morality as a condition of employment.

Take the Lead

One way to prevent the vicious New Rules from taking over the process of selecting our leaders is for journalists to blaze away at keyhole journalism. Another way is for voters to express their repugnance by writing to editors and sending money to targets.

The most effective immediate way is for potential leaders to take the lead. That means having the wit to field embarrassing questions, the wisdom to respond to profound questions, and the courage to invoke the go-to-hell rule on intimate personal questions.

"As it is used most of the time, TV tends to transform politics . . . into show business."

Campaign Advertising Is Harmful

Tom Wicker and Pat M. Holt

Candidates for high level office, such as governor, senator, and president, are increasingly using thirty-second television advertising as their principal means of communicating to voters. In Part I of the following viewpoint, Tom Wicker criticizes these spots as superficial, expensive, and often vindictive. In Part II, Pat Holt expresses concern that candidates' continued reliance on television advertising is alienating voters and causing low turnout. Wicker is a syndicated columnist with *The New York Times*. Holt is a Washington-based writer on foreign affairs.

As you read, consider the following questions:

1. According to Wicker, how does negative campaigning distort the issues?
2. What does Wicker think is the best way to curtail negative campaign advertising?
3. In what way does Holt think media consultants have failed in advising candidates on how to use television?

Tom Wicker, "The Road Not Taken," *The New York Times,* October 24, 1987. Copyright © 1987 by The New York Times Company. Reprinted by permission.
Pat M. Holt, "TV Campaigning: The Tail Wagging the Dog," *The Christian Science Monitor,* November 5, 1986. Reprinted with the author's permission.

I

Negative campaigning permits the none-too-subtle suggestion that an unmarried opponent may be a homosexual. By such lights, a candidate who refuses a urinalysis test may be a drug addict or peddler. President Reagan has urged Republicans to imply that anyone who opposes his S.D.I. has no stomach for "defending America."

Worse than Mudslinging

Don't confuse all this with traditional mudslinging. The stuff flying through the political air not only is smellier than that; today's guttersniping is doubly repellent—perhaps doubly lethal—because it's carried farther along the low road, with greater force and to more voters, by the candidates' use of television, primarily the 30-second spot.

To broadcast a multiplicity of these, contemporary candidates have to raise astronomical sums of money—often from special interests. But 30-second spots—which make up virtually the whole of many campaigns—convey no more useful or reliable information than, say, one of those commercials in which male-bonded yuppies or superannuated jocks extol the virtues of beer guzzling.

TV stations can't reject even false ads in which the sponsoring candidate's face or voice appears. But the skeptical viewer has no ready means to check on the so-called facts supposedly backing the charges these slippery spots wisp across his or her consciousness. The negative spot usually gets answered only by a negative spot from the other side; and sometimes the latter is less an answer than a countercharge:

"My opponent went to church only four Sundays out of a total of 52 opportunities last year."

"My church-going record is being outrageously distorted by a man who keeps a copy of the Meese Commission Report on Pornography in a plain brown wrapper in his desk drawer."

Voters Can Stop It

Does negative campaigning work? That depends on the public. If a candidate out-negs his opponent and wins, his tactics obviously succeed. But if voters want to put an end to all this electronic political assassination, they can stop voting for people who rely too sleazily on the tactic; or they can make a judgment that the least offender is the best bet. . . . Candidates will not for long keep doing things that don't win elections.

The worst remedy would be some kind of law to forbid or penalize negative spots—not only because of the difficulty of defining permissible limits, but because even the most odoriferous political discourse is a kind of speech and expression, and thus is properly protected by the First Amendment.

II

If the next few elections continue the trend of the last few, our political system may become unworkable. This lament has nothing to do with who wins and who loses elections; it has to do, rather, with the deterioration of the process itself.

The most striking and disturbing aspect of this is the degradation of political discourse. Enormous amounts of money are spent in efforts by talented people to compress complex issues into 30-second television spots. Most of the time what comes out on the screen has less to do with issues than with the perfidy or personal habits of the opposing candidate.

A good many politicians don't like to campaign this way with

The vast television political-campaign wasteland.

Paul Conrad. © 1986, Los Angeles Times. Reprinted by permission.

negative advertising, but their media consultants and campaign strategists tell them it works. And so it does, with discouraging frequency. Political advertising campaigns on television "might be dishonest," one TV reporter said, "but they're really neat."

This is the kind of cynicism which, if unchecked, will ultimately corrode and corrupt the whole political process. It is the glorification of imagery at the expense of substance. . . .

Turning Off Voters

There is evidence that perhaps growing numbers of people are finding political campaigns boring, confusing, offensive, or all of the above. One piece of this evidence is declining voter turnout. This public disgust may be what it takes to change the downward trend in the process and give more point to our political life.

It would be an enormous improvement if ways could be found to shorten campaigns. How do the British manage to compress into a month what takes us a year or two—or in the case of the presidency, more? Sure, we are a bigger country with more people who need to get the message—or image—but does it really take as long as we spend on it?

The length of campaigns and the perceived necessity to saturate the airwaves with scurrilous statements about the other candidate introduce another corrupting element—money. There has been enough hand wringing and pointing with alarm over this problem. It is admittedly complicated, but hardly more complicated than the tax reform or immigration reform that Congress summoned the political ingenuity to get done.

We are not going back to the campaign style of the Lincoln-Douglas debates. Television is here to stay; but despite the media consultants, campaign strategists, and pollsters it has spawned, we have not learned to use it to improve and civilize and sharpen our political discourse. There is nothing inherent in the medium that dictates the present state of affairs. On the contrary, there are examples—most of them provided by public broadcasting, but some by the commercial networks—of how good it could be.

The Tail Wagging the Dog

But as it is used most of the time, TV tends to transform politics—and journalism, too, for that matter—into show business. The tail is wagging the dog. Politicians are no longer in control of the process. They don't use television; television uses them. Again, we go back to the emphasis on imagery at the expense of substance. The presumed experts say this is what grabs attention. Maybe. But could it be that what the experts really mean is that it is easier for them, that it doesn't take as much effort, to deal with image than with substance?

"Political television does not manipulate the electorate in a new, pernicious way; it mainly spreads the candidate's message more widely."

Campaign Advertising Is Not Harmful

Edwin Diamond and Stephen Bates

In the following viewpoint, Edwin Diamond and Stephen Bates argue that the negative effects of television advertising are exaggerated. They contend that political television ads can be used to convey important information about candidates and issues. Television audiences, according to Diamond and Bates, can be trusted to view political advertising skeptically, and not be manipulated by it. Diamond is a professor of journalism at New York University and writes about the media for *New York* magazine. Stephen Bates is a free-lance writer in Cambridge, Massachusetts.

As you read, consider the following questions:

1. What reasons do the authors give for the decline of voter participation in elections?
2. According to Diamond and Bates, why is there little substance contained in most thirty-second spot advertisements?
3. Why do the authors believe that audiences can be trusted to critically evaluate the political television ads they see?

Edwin Diamond and Stephen Bates, *The Spot: The Rise of Political Advertising on Television.* Cambridge, MA: The MIT Press, 1984. Copyright © 1984 by The Massachusetts Institute of Technology.

121

Some critics argue that, total spending levels aside, campaigns spend too much on television. But, viewing a campaign as an educational process, TV is a good buy in political campaigns when compared to alternatives. By one estimate, reaching a TV viewer in 1983 cost less than half a cent, reaching the same person by a newspaper ad cost one and a half cents, and reaching the same person by direct mail cost around twenty-five cents. . . . We believe that restricting or abolishing polispots [political TV ads] would by itself not reduce overall spending levels. The money would go into other, less efficient forms of communication.

Reduced Political Participation

Turnout in presidential elections has declined in every election since 1960; only 53.9 percent of eligible citizens voted in 1980. This is the same period when the amount of money spent on television political advertising has tripled (in constant dollars). The national and the big state campaigns have taken money from participation-oriented activities such as canvassing and phone banks and put it into political spots. But it is extremely difficult to untangle the various factors that may relate to voting decline. There is evidence, for example, that other forms of political participation, such as letter writing, petition signing, and protesting, have increased while voting has gone down—people may be turning to other means of political expression. Some consultants we interviewed, notably Eddie Mahe, argue that the decline in voting is more apparent than real, a temporary artifact of the demography of the country. In the 1960s and 1970s the baby-boom generation reached voting age and reduced turnout figures (a reduction that increased when the voting age was lowered from twenty-one to eighteen, swelling the ranks of younger voters), because young people traditionally vote at a lower rate than older people. As that population bulge grows older, by this reasoning, voting turnouts will begin to increase. Still others argue that television campaigns alert apolitical people to the major event of an election and get them to come out; thus Nixon's media blitz of 1968 has been credited with sending poorer, less-educated Democratic voters to the polls. Perhaps, too, nonvoting may be an implicit declaration of satisfaction with the status quo. Or perhaps nonvoting reflects the judgment that candidates are indistinguishable. Jesse Jackson's early 1984 successes showed that blacks will register and vote when they perceive that a candidacy represents them. Television has been blamed for a variety of developments in American society. But correlation—the simultaneous expansion of television and of nonvoting—does not indicate causation. For now, at least, the vote is still out on whether media campaigns have contributed significantly to lower voter turnouts. . . .

The case about debasing frequently focuses on the brevity of spots: What can possibly be told in thirty seconds? In our studies of over 650 such spots, we found that a great deal can be said, though relatively few candidates do so. Straightforward positions can be made. Eisenhower's promise to go to Korea took less than thirty seconds. So did McGovern's promise to end the Vietnam War. John Deardourff, tired of the debasing criticism, once wrote this script as an exercise:

> I believe that the question of abortion is one that ought to be reserved exclusively to a woman and her doctor. I favor giving women the unfettered right to abortion. I also favor the federal funding of abortions through Medicaid for poor women as an extension of that right to an abortion, and I oppose any statutory or constitutional limitations on that right.

As Deardourff explained, "That's twenty-four seconds. I don't know how much more one needs to know about that subject in order to form an opinion if that's an issue about which you're concerned."

Media Campaigns Are Here To Stay

Like it or not, media campaigns are here to stay. It borders on the Luddite to argue that candidates should spend their time mingling with voters instead of communicating with them by television. Besides, mingling isn't that easy because practically no one except the party faithful shows up at campaign rallies these days. Not surprisingly, candidates tend to emphasize TV ads, particularly in heavily populated states where they would cross paths with only a minuscule percentage of the electorate even if they tried.

Fred Barnes, *The New Republic*, November 24, 1986.

Most campaigns avoid such specifics, but that has less to do with the thirty-second spot format than with campaign strategy. John Lindsay's 1972 presidential campaign ran a thirty-second spot in Florida that gave the candidate's position on, among other issues, gun control (for), abortion (for), and school prayer (against). "He probably lost the entire population of Florida in that one spot," Lindsay's media manager, David Garth, later said. The risks and benefits of an issues strategy have little to do with the polispots form per se. Pretelevision, those same voters would have found something to dislike in the candidate's positions—if, that is, they learned about them to begin with. As for the length of spots, Carroll Newton, the ad agency executive who worked in the Eisenhower campaigns and the first Nixon campaign, once calculated that a half-hour speech would lose a third of the time slot's normal audience; a fifteen-minute speech would lose a quarter of the audience; a five-minute speech would lose from 5

123

to 10 percent; and a thirty- or sixty-second spot would lose nothing. Long form telecasts usually end up preaching to the already converted—which is important, but not the only goal. . . .

A Sophisticated Audience

In the end, still, we are willing to leave the polispots and the media campaigns to the knowing judgment of the audience. The typical thirty-five-year-old American has been watching television for three decades now and has been through more than a dozen political campaigns as a television consumer. The majority of the audience belongs to the party of skeptics, and not just about political promises; a 1977 Harris poll showed forty-six percent of those surveyed assenting to the statement that most or all ads on TV are "seriously misleading." Narrowcasting on cable and high-tech interactive systems will not alter that balance of doubt.

The media managers line up with us on this point. "As politically unsophisticated as voters are, they are extremely sophisticated as TV viewers," says Ken Swope. David Sawyer concurs: "There's no way you can manipulate the voters. There's no way you can go back now and talk about a government as decent and beautiful as the American people. There's no way you can go back now and show the candidate wandering down the beach, with his jacket over his shoulder and a dog running by his side. Those are clichés from the period when political television was naive. People now are looking with sophistication at your messages. Put out a message to con them, and they'll figure it out like that." Of course it is still possible to run unfair, or scurrilous, or racist campaigns on television—just as it has always been possible to run them in newspapers, leaflets, and speeches. Political television does not manipulate the electorate in a new, pernicious way; it mainly spreads the candidate's message more widely and more efficiently. The message still must travel past watchful eyes—the press's, the opposition's, and the voters'.

Distinguishing Between Fact and Opinion

This activity is designed to help develop the critical thinking skill of distinguishing between fact and opinion. Consider the following statement as an example: "The television networks carry live coverage of the voting returns on election night." This is an easily verifiable statement. But consider this statement: "The networks' election night coverage trivializes the election process by treating the election as a sporting event." Contending that the networks trivialize the election process is the author's opinion. A critic of the media might agree, while a broadcaster probably would not.

In distinguishing between fact and opinion, it is important to recognize that not all statements of fact are true. They may appear to be true but some are based on inaccurate or false information. For this activity, however, we are concerned with understanding the difference between those statements which appear to be factual and those which appear to be based primarily on opinion.

The following statements are related to topics covered in this chapter. Consider each statement carefully. *Mark O for any statement you believe is an opinion or interpretation of facts. Mark F for any statement you believe is a fact. Mark U if you are uncertain.*

If you are doing this activity as a member of a class or group, compare your answers with those of other class or group members. Be able to defend your answers. You may discover that others will come to different conclusions than you. Listening to the reasons others present for their answers may give you valuable insights in distinguishing between fact and opinion.

> O = *opinion*
> F = *fact*
> U = *uncertain*

1. The public's curiosity about who is winning is real and the news media should try to satisfy it.

2. Presidential primary voters get 90% of their election information from the news media.

3. Anything that keeps a politician humble and slightly unnerved is healthy for democracy.

4. Only 54 percent of eligible citizens voted in the 1980 elections.

5. Thousands of dollars are spent in efforts by talented people to compress complex issues into 30-second television spots.

6. Dwight D. Eisenhower's wartime affair with Kay Summersby Morgan did not become public knowledge until 30 years after the fact.

7. Privacy for candidates should stop where wealth and health begin.

8. Candidates now tailor their comments for the short sound-bites usable on the nightly news shows.

9. The Constitution does not require chastity of those who seek to be president.

10. The typical thirty-five-year-old American has been watching television for three decades.

11. As politically unsophisticated as voters are, they are extremely sophisticated as television viewers.

12. Thirty-second advertisements convey little useful or reliable information.

13. Many reporters allowed themselves to be gulled by the electronic facades of candidates.

14. About $350 million was spent on political television advertising during the 1986 elections.

15. There are more reporters from national publications covering the Iowa caucuses today than in 1976.

Periodical Bibliography

The following articles have been selected to supplement the diverse views presented in this chapter.

Fred Barnes — "Worthy Mud," *The New Republic*, November 24, 1986.

William F. Buckley Jr. — "Hart's Problem and Ours," *National Review*, June 5, 1987.

Commonweal — "Gary-kari," May 22, 1987.

Harold Evans — "Free Speech and Free Air," *U.S. News & World Report*, May 11, 1987.

Edward O. Fritts — "Free Time Is Not the Answer," *U.S. News & World Report*, June 1, 1987.

Meg Greenfield — "Private Lives, Public Values," *Newsweek*, May 18, 1987.

Hendrik Hertzberg — "Sluicegate," *The New Republic*, June 1, 1987.

Nicholas von Hoffman — "Peephole Journalism: Should the Press Play Vice Cop?" *The Nation*, June 20, 1987.

Victor Kamber — "TV News as Political Kingmaker," *U.S. News & World Report*, June 15, 1987.

National Review — "New Morality, New Journalism," June 5, 1987.

Jeffrey L. Pasley — "Postmodern Hustle," *The New Republic*, November 3, 1986.

Nelson W. Polsby — "Was Hart's Life Unfairly Probed? The Public Interest Outweighs Privacy," *The New York Times*, May 6, 1987.

Steven V. Roberts — "Politicking Goes High-Tech," *The New York Times Magazine*, November 2, 1986.

Patricia Sellers — "The Selling of the President in '88," *Fortune*, December 21, 1987.

Time — "Private Life, Public Office," May 18, 1987.

George F. Will — "So Much Cash, So Few Ideas," *Newsweek*, November 6, 1986.

William Zimmerman — "On Negative Ads," *The New York Times*, November 13, 1986.

4 CHAPTER

How Should US Presidents Be Elected?

AMERICA'S
ELECTIONS

Chapter Preface

In the debate over the presidential election process one question remains central: How much influence should the general public have in choosing a president?

Some people believe the public has too much influence in choosing candidates. They believe that the current methods—choosing candidates through primary and caucus systems—do not serve the voters or the parties well. According to these critics, voters in primary elections are unduly influenced by the news media. Media hype also gives an advantage to winners of the first contests. Therefore, if an obscure candidate with little experience wins early contests, voters may favor that candidate despite his or her lack of qualifications. These critics suggest that instead of letting voters in primary elections choose candidates, party leaders and elected officials should be the ones to choose the candidates. They argue that candidates chosen by other politicans would be more likely to have the experience and prestige necessary to work with other government leaders in making policy.

Advocates of the primary system disagree. They argue that in a democracy, voters, not party leaders, must make the choice about candidates. Although these supporters agree that the process may get distorted by press coverage of early primaries, they believe that this problem can be solved by modifying the primary schedule. From their point of view, the greater the role played by voters in choosing a party's candidate, the better.

The viewpoints in the following chapter present debates over how the US president is chosen and who is most qualified to do the choosing.

"Revisions can make the [primary] system more rational, less beholden to separate groups, and more reflective of the national will."

The Primary System Should Be Reformed

Charles T. Manatt

Charles T. Manatt believes that more voters should have a say in the process of choosing a presidential nominee. He points to the disproportionate amount of time and money presidential candidates spend wooing voters in Iowa and New Hampshire, the first states to choose delegates for party conventions. In the following viewpoint, he recommends a streamlined system of primaries, in which a larger number and wider variety of voters would play a role in choosing delegates. Manatt is a lawyer in Washington, DC, and a former chairman of the Democratic National Committee.

As you read, consider the following questions:

1. Why does Manatt think that restricting primaries and allowing party leadership to decide who the presidential candidate should be is not a good idea?
2. According to the author, why must Congress intervene if there is to be effective reform of the primary system?
3. How does Manatt propose to have voters from places other than Iowa and New Hampshire have a greater say in who will be the nominee?

Charles T. Manatt, "A New Primary System," in *Before Nomination: Our Primary Problems.* Washington, DC: American Enterprise Institute, 1985. Copyright © 1985 Gerald R. Ford Foundation.

The 1968 [Democratic] convention provided the spark that set off a chain reaction of reform that has not yet spent itself. In 1968 there was an impression, right or wrong, that the eventual nominee, Hubert Humphrey, who had not entered a single primary, was not the popular choice. The critics could point to some glaring examples of apparent unfairness: a Georgia delegation picked personally by the governor, with no democratic participation or recourse; a Texas delegation with the unit rule, forcing the opponents of the Vietnam War within that delegation to cast a vote in favor of it; other delegations selected far in advance of the convention, long before the campaigns of Robert Kennedy and Eugene McCarthy and even longer before the withdrawal of Lyndon Johnson.

Added to these pressures was the rising call for the empowerment of new forces—with blacks now joined by Hispanics, the young, and women, who were starting to express a new and powerful consciousness of their own identity. To conciliate these forces and as part of the effort to rescue his candidacy from the chaos of the Chicago convention, Humphrey agreed to establish a commission to rewrite the rules for 1972 and beyond.

Reform Not an Accident

This history points to an important insight: the reforms were not an accident but a result of irrepressible events and broader trends. It also suggests that although the rules can be—and have been—repeatedly amended, the reforms cannot, in their fundamental aspects, be rolled back. The Republican party, which was not the crucible of these changes, has adopted many of them. One reason is that state laws that apply to both parties were adopted to accommodate the Democratic reforms. The other reason, more pervasive and powerful, is that the rules changes reflected real changes in American society—changes that either party could ignore only at its peril. At the 1984 Dallas convention, Republicans denounced quotas—and then celebrated the fact that nearly half their delegates were women.

There are two fashionable reactions to this period of reform, both of which I reject. I do not accept the notion that the old system produced better nominees and somehow did so precisely because of its rules. Any such argument depends on selective history and on the assumption that the nominating process can be made into a special preserve, sealed off from the mood and movements of the times. The old system produced Harding and Nixon as well as Eisenhower and Kennedy. We Democrats had fewer chances to make mistakes in those years not because the rules protected us but because the unprecedented four terms of Franklin Roosevelt prevented us for a long time from nominating someone else. Who imagined that the old rules could have survived the transformation of modern communications and con-

131

sciousness? After Watergate could the Republicans—or the Democrats—really have chosen their nominee in a smoke-filled room? If the choice in 1984 had been left to party leaders and not to primaries, would it have been any different, given that so many of those leaders had already decided by the end of 1983 to endorse Mondale?

Just as I reject the notion that the old was better, I also reject the fashionable argument that what we have now is good enough and that it cannot or should not be improved. Revisions in the rules will not, on our side, cure all that ails the Democratic party or, on the other side, alter the underlying factors that could undermine the present Republican success. But revisions can make the system more rational, less beholden to separate groups, and more reflective of the national will. . . .

Congressional Action Needed

Together both parties can shape and seek changes based on merit and not on the calculus of individual interest. They can move in Congress, in ways that I will outline, to mandate steps toward goals that virtually everyone professes but no one so far seems able to achieve.

The critical cause of our failure to achieve them is that we have considered the question chiefly in the context of party commis-

" THAT ONE'S FOR ELECTION YEARS...."

John Trever. Reprinted with permission.

sions, which have largely been dominated by the representatives and adherents of prospective candidates. Congress offers a different forum, which can focus on broader purposes and can invoke effective powers of enforcement. Congressional action not only is the best way to deal with the length of the process but may be the only way. Federal legislation can deny matching funds to candidates who violate federal guidelines.

Those guidelines should set primaries on four dates—the first or second Tuesdays in March, April, May, and June. Caucuses could be held any time in the week following the primaries. To avoid the distortion of having all the states in a single region vote on the same day, without the balancing effect of a more representative diversity, Congress should consider time-zone primaries. Which time zone went first and which followed in any given year should be determined by lottery. For the 1988 campaign, the lottery should be held in December 1986. Any candidate who participated in a nonapproved delegate selection process held outside this system would lose federal matching funds.

More Coherent Dialogue

As a former national chairman, I saw what happened when we tried, on our own, to shorten the process for 1984. We made some progress—Iowa came five weeks later than in 1980 and New Hampshire a week later—but it proved virtually impossible to do more, especially to eliminate the special status of the two states. At least one candidate will always parade as their defender, and the others cannot afford to be seen as the ones who tried to deny Iowa or New Hampshire its rightful priority. So those states can pick their dates, regardless of party rules, and assume that by the time the convention comes, the winning candidate will not let it refuse to seat their delegates. Imagine the plight of candidates who had to campaign in the New Hampshire primary after trying to abolish it. The issue would not be the economy, or Central America, or new ideas, or old values. It would be why they tried to deprive the state of its place in the news and its lion's share of campaign revenues.

This is no way to pick a president. In 1984 candidates had to pay, according to a price list, to put up banners or posters at a New Hampshire party event. They even had to pay a price to speak. Perhaps there is a rough justice in that, at least for some political speakers we have all heard; but such practices degrade not only the candidates but the process. They do not advance the cause of picking a nominee; they exploit it.

New Hampshire makes no more sense as the first primary for selecting a Democratic nominee than Massachusetts would as the first primary for the Republicans. And although I was raised in Iowa and I will certainly hear about this when I go back, Iowa too has no special claim and deserves no automatic priority.

The system I suggest has the added advantage of inviting a more coherent and less debilitating dialogue. In 1983 and 1984 we saw an increasing proliferation of joint appearances, debates, and speech contests, often used by state parties as fund-raising vehicles. Too readily these events tempt candidates, especially those who are behind, to launch the kind of attacks that almost fatally weaken a likely nominee for the coming campaign. What we need is a greater certainty of debates in the general election and greater control over the number and intensity of exchanges during the primary period. Perhaps, as part of the reform I have proposed, the national parties should sponsor four debates in 1988—on the four Saturdays or Sundays before the designated primary dates.

Nominees Picked Too Early

Voters in New Hampshire and a few other early primaries often virtually get the right to nominate their party's candidate. Candidates who do not do well in these early stages get discouraged and their financial contributors and volunteers desert them. In practice, voters in later states often get presented with just one or possibly one and a half surviving candidates—which leaves many voters in California or Colorado feeling that they have been both cheated and disenfranchised. The final result is that, in most presidential years, the nominees of both major parties are decided much too early in the process.

Thomas E. Cronin and Robert D. Loevy, *The Presidential Nominating Process*, vol. I, 1983.

Any plan to shorten the process will be only half successful if it fails to deal with the straw polls, which foster an early start and a relentlessly paced campaign. Here, again, I believe that the matching funds system provides a mechanism for reform. The law should be amended so that any contributions raised before October 1 in the year preceding the primaries will not be eligible for federal matching. Candidates could raise enough to sustain a preprimary operation, but they would be unlikely to raise more and more unmatchable money to compete in unsanctioned straw polls.

To me October 1 is certainly a reasonable date to start matching. A quarter of a century ago, John Kennedy was counted as an early entry because he announced his candidacy on January 3, 1960, and the crucial organizing meeting of his campaign was held in October 1959. Perhaps we cannot restore that sense of proportion to the process; but at least we can moderate a situation in which we are perilously close to the moment when, in Adlai Stevenson's words, the nominee will be "the last survivor."

"The primaries . . . have assumed a dominant role in the nominating process, though they are clearly unfit for it."

The Primary System Should Be Weakened

Donald L. Robinson

The majority of states elect convention delegates through voter primaries or through caucuses that are open to the public. In the following viewpoint, Donald L. Robinson argues that the parties rely too much on primaries in deciding who their candidate for president should be. He contends that party leadership needs to play a more decisive role in choosing the parties' candidates. Without the support of the party leadership, Robinson believes a presidential candidate cannot be successful once in office. Robinson is a professor of government at Smith College in Massachusetts.

As you read, consider the following questions:

1. What example does Robinson use to show that the primary system does not always choose the most popular candidate?
2. According to Robinson, why does the primary system strengthen the individual candidate at the expense of his or her party?
3. Why does the author think the primary system does not encourage good government?

Excerpts from *"To the Best of My Ability"* by Donald L. Robinson are reprinted by permission of W.W. Norton & Company, Inc. Copyright © 1987 by Donald L. Robinson.

In recent years presidential elections have failed to produce a durable sense of political renewal. The active, public part of the campaign stretches on for nearly a year, and long before it is over, both the candidates and the public have been exhausted and disgusted by the spectacle. The primaries, once a useful means for informing and checking the judgments of party leaders about the popularity of candidates, have assumed a dominant role in the nominating process, though they are clearly unfit for it. Therefore, few voters participate in them, and the relative influence of states is so capricious that the results are an unreliable guide even to a candidate's popularity, much less his fitness for the nation's most demanding job. Yet because the primaries are dominant, the party conventions, once great festivals of democracy, have been reduced to second-rate television entertainment. Most delegates, chosen for their loyalty to particular candidates rather than for their own political skills, are unknown to one another and unsuited to deliberate creatively on their party's nominee, and without this dramatic element the festivities become boring and are virtually devoid of political meaning.

Candidates Too Independent

As for the general election, it becomes a contest between two ad hoc organizations with only tenuous connections to political party organizations. Despite strenuous efforts by candidates and campaign organizations, including the preparation and publication of innumerable issue papers and party platforms, and despite earnest work by reporters and commentators—or perhaps *because* of these massive efforts—the public remains confused about the significance of the choice it must make, as far as future policies are concerned. Thus, the mandate is blurred. Candidates for president do not totally ignore their party affiliations. They may seek to quicken partisan loyalties and to use partisan organizations— but only to the extent that they do not interfere with prior commitments and strategic objectives. As a result, party leaders cannot claim any leverage over the candidates on behalf of ongoing organizational commitments, and party labels provide unreliable cues for voters. The absence of loyalty to an ongoing organization obscures the meaning of popular choice, and after the election ordinary citizens become spectators while the winning candidate develops his own interpretation of the "mandate." . . .

The United States now has "a government of strangers," a phenomenon deeply rooted in the post-World War II electoral system. The estrangement is pervasive. Delegates to national nominating conventions are no longer linked even by a network of party leaders who are familiar to one another. Most delegates are strangers even to the candidate they support. They know only his television persona. The strangeness extends throughout the election, and beyond. During the campaign local party workers are shoved aside by the candidate's lieutenants, people sent in from distant precincts and states. When presidents first gather their newly appointed cabinets around a table at the White House, the room is full of strangers.

This is a relatively recent phenomenon. Its roots go back to 1952 and Eisenhower, who won the nomination by successfully challenging the regular delegations committed to "Mr. Republican," Senator Robert Taft of Ohio, and then proceeded to conduct his general election campaign through an organization called Citizens for Eisenhower, rather than the Republican National Committee.

Don Wright, The Miami News. Reprinted with permission.

The changes did not gather momentum and become permanently institutionalized until the cultural revolution of the 1960s. The civil rights and antiwar movements produced demands that institutions open up to broader participation. Such demands fell heaviest on institutions that were perceived as abusing their authority. The Democratic party, personified by President Johnson, came under heavy attack by the advocates of "participatory democracy" at its 1968 national convention. The convention responded in part by promising that the party would appoint a commission to "reform" the process for choosing delegates to its national convention.

A disarming but astute senator from South Dakota, George McGovern, agreed to chair the commission that inherited this task.

Called the Commission on Party Structure and Delegate Selection, it took its mandate from a resolution of the 1968 convention which directed that all Democratic voters be given an opportunity to participate in the selection of delegates to the 1972 convention.

The report of the McGovern Commission, issued in April 1970, had an apocalyptic tone. The Democratic party, it said, offered the only hope for orderly, peaceful change in America. If it failed to reform, people demanding change would have no alternative but to join splinter parties or engage in the "anti-politics of the street." Piecemeal concession would not suffice. For the party to survive, it would be necessary "to open the door to all Democrats who seek a voice in their party's most important decision: the choice of its presidential nominee." The commission issued guidelines calling on state parties to take "affirmative steps" to encourage the representation of minority groups, young people, and women "in reasonable relationship to the group's presence in the population of the state" (what came to be called quotas); to prohibit ex officio delegates (that is, those who became delegates by virtue of holding office as a governor or senator, or whatever); and to forbid the unit rule as an infringement on the conscience of individual delegates.

Primaries Proliferate

In retrospect, it is worth noting that the commission did not require or even urge the adoption of primaries as a means for achieving these ends, although in a brief, concluding section of its final report, summarizing progress to date in responding to its guidelines, the commission saluted several states that had already adopted primaries.

In any case, primaries did proliferate in the ensuing years. According to Howard Reiter, whereas in 1968 fourteen states used them to select or bind delegates to national conventions, by 1976 twenty-seven states did so, and by 1980, thirty-four of them. The consequence was to shift the center of gravity at the conventions. Whereas in 1968 only about one-third of the delegates were chosen or bound by primaries, by 1976 nearly three-quarters were. To shift the onus for complying with the Democratic party's new rules, political leaders in several states had seen to it that voters themselves could choose the delegates in primaries. . . .

The main effect of the McGovern Commission guidelines was to change the traditional role and character of presidential primaries. From the beginning of the twentieth century, when primaries were first introduced as checks on the power of bosses to dictate the nomination, they had been few in number, and their influence on the nomination had been informal and special. They gave opportunity to Adlai Stevenson to demonstrate that he could win in the South, to Dwight Eisenhower to prove that his popularity as a war hero had electoral value, and to John Kennedy to show that Bible Belt Protestants would vote for him. Never before the McGovern reforms, however, did a candidate win a nomination solely, or even mainly, by winning a string of primaries. Estes Kefauver tried in 1952 and 1956; but there were not enough of them, and their outcomes were not binding. Kefauver's victories in several primaries failed to convince the party's leaders that he was fit for the presidency; at the 1952 convention they made their choice of Adlai Stevenson over New York's Governor Averell Harriman.

Restore Power to Party Leaders

Something must be done to bring the campaign season back within rational and endurable limits, and to recreate the possibility for the parties to choose those who have better qualifications for the presidency than simply wanting it.

This certainly will mean putting power back into the smoke-filled rooms and restoring power to party leadership and the party conventions. It could mean giving senators and congressmen formal roles in party leadership and at the conventions. . . .

There is no reason Americans have to go on haphazardly and, too often in recent years, disastrously selecting the president by a process that amounts to a media-man version of the old American bamboozle and snake-oil swindle, with the citizenry in the role of rube. We can't afford it.

William Pfaff, *Minneapolis Star Tribune*, October 17, 1987.

The campaign of 1972 was the first in which a candidate parlayed primary victories into a presidential nomination. The beneficiary—many thought not coincidentally—was George McGovern. The situation was ironic. A process that was intended to allow popular choice to triumph over the dictates of bosses resulted in the nomination of a man who had consistently trailed his rivals in surveys of public opinion. In a January sampling McGovern had the support of only 3 percent of voters who identified themselves as Democrats. Even after his victories in the primaries McGovern had the support of only about 30 percent of the Democrats nationwide.

The ensuing general election showed that the 1972 Democratic Convention had failed to unite the party. McGovern got one of the lowest percentage of votes ever won by a Democratic nominee. Despite the fact that Democrats outnumbered Republicans that year by a 43 to 28 percent margin, McGovern got only 38 percent of the vote to Nixon's 61 percent. The distaste of the electorate for the choice between McGovern and Nixon was indicated by the fact that the turnout of eligible voters outside the South was the lowest since 1824, excepting the elections of 1920 and 1924, the first two in which women were eligible to vote.

Yet for better or worse most of the large states were committed to binding primary elections by the mid-1970s. In fact, when Senator Edward M. Kennedy argued in 1980 that delegates, even those chosen in primaries, should be free at the convention to vote their personal preferences (an interpretation in accord with the McGovern Commission guidelines), the delegates, most of them pledged to support President Carter, said no. Delegates, they said, like federal electors, were not chosen to exercise judgment. They were chosen to carry out the will of the voters. Thus were primaries controlling the nominating process.

Party Leaders Shut Out

One other aspect of these developments needs to be underlined: the abrupt dismissal of senators from the nominating process, particularly by the Democratic party, and their replacement by "strangers." Between 1952 and 1968 an average of more than 70 percent of incumbent Democratic senators became delegates to their party's national conventions. In 1972 that number was cut in half. In 1976 it was 18 percent, and in 1980, 13.8 percent. Meanwhile, the percentage of delegates attending their first national convention rose from 54 percent in 1964 to 87 percent in 1980.

By the early 1980s these developments in the nominating process were amply satisfying the framers' hope that the presidency would be separated from the rest of the system. The logic of the constitutional system, coupled with the insistence of modern culture on direct democracy, had triumphed almost completely over the impulse of politicians to bind the elements of the system together. . . .

None of the reforms of the past century was adopted in the interest of enhancing a successful candidate's capacity to govern. In fact, reformers have almost always stressed the importance of reinforcing a candidate's *independence* from those whose cooperation would be essential for effective government. And they have left us with a process unrecommended by success in any previous system, anywhere in the world. No other nation in the world, none ever, anywhere, has chosen its candidates for leader of the government by a direct popular election. . . .

The drive to democratize the government by streamlining presidential elections had impatiently swept aside all barriers— except the apathy and cynicism produced by a system that promises more, in terms of democratic control, than it can possibly deliver.

140

"There are good reasons to stay with the current [primary system] arrangement."

The Primary System Should Remain Unchanged

Michael Nelson

In the following viewpoint, Michael Nelson argues that the current presidential nomination process produces candidates who are experienced in building broad coalitions, are adept in dealing with the mass media, and have knowledge of the diverse problems of different areas of the country. He believes that these are skills that are necessary for being an effective president. Therefore, he contends that there is little reason to make dramatic changes in the way parties choose their presidential candidates. Nelson is a political science professor at Vanderbilt University in Tennessee.

As you read, consider the following questions:

1. Why does the author believe that the reforms in the presidential nomination process have not weakened the political parties?
2. According to Nelson, how has the power structure in Washington changed in the last thirty years? How does the reformed election process complement this change?
3. What weaknesses does Nelson admit the current process has? Why doesn't he think these flaws outweigh the advantages of the present system?

Michael Nelson, "The Case for the Current Presidential Nomination Process," in *Before Nomination: Our Primary Problems.* Washington, DC: American Enterprise Institute, 1985. Copyright © 1985 Gerald R. Ford Foundation.

The current process by which Americans nominate their parties' candidates for president is the product of nearly two centuries of historical evolution and two decades of deliberate procedural reform. It can be judged successful because it satisfies reasonably well [these] criteria by which any presidential nominating process may be judged:

• Does the process strengthen or weaken the two major parties, which our political system relies on to provide some measure of coherence to a constitutionally fragmented government?

• Does the process foster or impede the selection of presidents who are suitably skilled for the office? . . .

Have the two major parties been weakened by the reforms of the presidential nominating process that were instituted by the McGovern-Fraser commission and its successors? Much scholarly talent and energy have been devoted to answering this question in the affirmative. Implicit in such analyses are the beliefs that the parties were basically strong before the post-1968 reforms and that they have been considerably weaker ever since. In truth, neither of these beliefs is fully accurate. The parties were in a state of decline during the 1950s and 1960s, a decline that has been arrested and in most cases reversed during the 1970s and 1980s, as the parties, aided by the reforms, have adapted to the changed social and political environment that underlay their decline. . . .

Party Loyalty Increasing

Americans are no longer as loyal to the parties as they were in the early 1950s, when modern survey research on voting behavior first took form. On this there is little room for dispute: voters are far less likely now than in the past to think of themselves as either Democrats or Republicans, to vote a straight-party ticket (even for presidential and House candidates), or to express a favorable evaluation of one or both political parties.

Natural though the tendency may be to explain dramatic changes by equally dramatic causes, one cannot attribute the decline of the party-in-the-electorate to the reform era that began in 1968. The largest falloff in party identification, which had remained steadily high through the 1950s and early 1960s, came between 1964 and 1966. An additional large drop occurred between 1970 and 1972, but since then the decline in party identification seems to have leveled off or even been reversed. The share of voters who evaluate at least one party favorably, which fell steadily during the 1960s, has stayed very close to 50 percent ever since, rising to 52 percent in 1984. Similarly, split-ticket voting, a more explicitly behavioral indicator of weak voter loyalty to the parties, underwent its greatest increases before the reform era and has declined since 1980. . . .

142

Marathon Runner

© Graham/Rothco.

Political parties in all their aspects—in the electorate, in government, and as organizations—were weakened during the 1950s and 1960s. . . . To recover and thrive the parties had to adapt. To adapt they had to accommodate the rise of four main groups: new-style voters, who by virtue of greater education and leisure no longer needed to depend on parties to order their choices in elections; amateur political activists who regarded the parties mainly as vehicles for political change; entrepreneurial candidates who had ceased to regard party fealty as the necessary or even the most desirable strategy for electoral success; and modern political tacticians who practiced the now essential crafts of polling, advertising, press relations, and fund raising. In sum, the reinvigoration of the parties would have to come on terms that accepted the "new politics" in both that label's common uses: policy as the basis for political participation, and modern campaign professionalism as the incentive to channel such participation through the parties.

The Post-1968 Reforms

What made the transformation and reinvigoration of the parties possible was the organizational and procedural fluidity that was hastened by the post-1968 reforms. Once the lingering hold of party professionals of the *ancien regime* on the nominating process was broken, the new groups of voters, activists, candidates, and campaign professionals were able to establish a new equilibrium of power within the parties that reflected the changed social and political realities. Republicans realized this first and strengthened their party by committing it to conservative political ideology and professional campaign services, which in turn tied the party-in-the-electorate, the party-in-government, and the party organization together. Democrats, preoccupied with the reform process more than with the fruits of reform, were slower to adapt. But, responding to the Republican party's success, they now seem to be following a parallel path: new policies and a new professionalism to rebuild the party. . . .

Many political analysts have argued vigorously that the influence of the presidential nominating process on the selection of suitably skilled presidents, like its influence on the parties, was benign before the post-1968 reforms were instituted but has been malignant ever since. "In the old way," according to [journalist David] Broder, "whoever wanted to run for president of the United States took a couple of months off from public service in the year of the presidential election and presented his credentials to the leaders of his party, who were elected officials, party officials, leaders of allied interest groups, and bosses in some cases. These people had known the candidate over a period of time and had carefully examined his work." As it happened, the qualities those political peers were looking for, argues political scientist Jeane Kirkpatrick, were the very qualities that make for good presidents: "the ability to deal with diverse groups, ability to work out compromises, and the ability to impress people who have watched a candidate over many years." In contrast, under the post-1968 rules, "the skills required to be successful in the nominating process are almost entirely irrelevant to, perhaps even negatively correlated with, the skills required to be successful at governing."

The "New" Washington

In a real sense, the old nominating process did work reasonably well to increase the chances of selecting skillful presidents. But then so does the new process. The difference underlying this similarity is the contrast between the political and social environment in which contemporary presidents must try to govern and the environment in which their predecessors as recently as the 1950s and 1960s had to operate.

Process Needs Stability

We should be careful lest our laudable enthusiasm for making things better lead us to urge the parties to constantly tinker with their procedures. This argument is something more than insisting we need to be sensitive to "the unintended consequences of purposive social action." It is also more than insisting upon the need to recognize that every system of presidential selection must have its own weaknesses and biases. It involves, especially, the judgment that there is a vital national interest in achieving order, stability, and predictability in election machinery. Electoral reform should be approached from a perspective that recognizes how important it is in this area to settle on something and stick with it.

Everett Carll Ladd, *Political Science Quarterly*, Fall 1987.

The contrast is most obvious and significant in the nation's capital. As Samuel Kernell notes, the "old" Washington that was described so accurately by Richard Neustadt in his 1960 success manual for presidents, *Presidential Power,* was "a city filled with hierarchies. To these hierarchies were attached leaders or least authoritative representatives"—committee chairmen and party leaders in Congress, press barons, umbrella-style interest groups that represented broad sectors such as labor, business, and agriculture, and so on. In this setting to lead was to bargain—the same political "whales," to use Harry MacPherson's term, who could thwart a president's desires could also satisfy them, and in the same way: by directing the activities of their associates and followers. Clearly a presidential nominating process that placed some emphasis on a candidate's ability to pass muster with Washington power brokers was functional for the governing system.

As the 1960s drew to a close, however, the same social and political changes—and some others as well—that were undermining the foundations of the old party system also were undermining the old ways of conducting the nation's business in Washington. The capital came under the intense and—to many elected politicians—alluring spotlight of television news; a more educated and active citizenry took its heightened policy concerns directly to government officials; interest group activity both flourished and fragmented; and careerism among members of Congress prompted a steady devolution of legislative power to individual representatives and senators and to proliferating committees and subcommittees. From the president's perspective this wave of decentralization meant that Washington had become "a city of free agents" in which "the number of exchanges necessary to secure others' support ha[d] increased dramatically."

What a President Needs

What skills do contemporary presidents need if they are to lead in this changed environment, or, to phrase the question more pertinently, what skills should the presidential nominating process foster? Two presidential leadership requirements are familiar and longstanding: first, a strategic sense of the public's disposition to be led during the particular term of office—an ability to sense, shape, and fulfill the historical possibilities of the time; second, some talent for the management of authority, both of lieutenants in the administration who can help the president form policy proposals and of the large organizations in the bureaucracy that are charged with implementing existing programs. Other skills required by presidents are more recent in origin, at least in the form they must take and their importance. Presidents must be able to present themselves and their policies to the public through rhetoric and symbolic action, especially on television. Because reelection-oriented members of Congress "are hypersensitive to anticipated constituent reaction," it is not surprising that the best predictor of a president's success with Congress is his standing in the public opinion polls. Finally, presidents need tactical skills of bargaining, persuasion, and other forms of political gamesmanship to maximize their support among other officials whose help they need to secure their purposes. But in the new Washington these tactical skills must be employed not merely or even mainly on the sort of old-style power brokers who used to be able to help presidents sustain reliable coalitions but on the many elements of a fragmented power system in which tactics must be improvised for new coalitions on each issue.

In several nonobvious and even inadvertent ways, the current nominating process rewards, perhaps requires, most of these skills. The process is, for would-be presidents, self-starting and complex. To a greater extent than ever before, candidates must raise money, develop appealing issues, devise shrewd campaign strategies, impress national political reporters, attract competent staff, and build active organizations largely on their own. They then must dance through a minefield of staggered and varied state primaries and caucuses, deciding and reevaluating weekly or even daily where to spend their time, money, and other resources. What better test of a president's ability to manage lieutenants and lead in a tactically skillful way in the equally complex, fragmented, and uncertain environment of modern Washington or, for that matter, the modern world?

No Better Alternative

What is left for capable politicians with substantial accomplishments but not national stature who want to "go national"? They can present themselves in long presidential campaigns where party activists and rank-and-file voters have ample opportunity to look them over; they must do their utmost to convince this jury they are qualified for the country's highest office. Would those of us who form the juries really want the campaigns to be shorter and otherwise less burdensome on these candidates? As the current campaign progresses, we have a chance to see presidential hopefuls not previously well known to us operate in a variety of contexts which—if not perfectly reflective of the demands of the presidency—unquestionably give us insight into their leadership ability, policy perspectives, personalities, and ethical judgment under pressure. The current credentialing system, based on extended campaign exposure, emerged when no satisfactory functional alternative could be found. It can be replaced only when and if such alternatives are put in place. No convincing practical alternative has been put forward.

Everett Carll Ladd, *The Christian Science Monitor*, September 15, 1987.

The fluidity of the current nominating process also has opened it to Washington "outsiders." This development, although much lamented by critics of the post-1968 reforms, has done nothing more than restore the traditional place of those who have served as state governors in the ranks of plausible candidates for the presidency, thus broadening the talent pool to include more than senators and vice-presidents. (From 1960 to 1972 every major party nominee for president was a senator or a vice-president who previously had been a senator.) As chief executives of their states, governors may be presumed to have certain skills in the management of large public bureaucracies that senators do not.

Self-presentational skills also are vital for candidates in the current nominating process—not just "looking good on television" but being able to persuade skeptical journalists and others to accept one's interpretation of the complex reality of the campaign. If it does nothing else, the endless contest, which carries candidates from place to place for months and months in settings that range from living rooms to stadiums, probably sensitizes candidates to citizens in ways that uniquely facilitate the choice of a president who has a strong strategic sense of his time.

No earthly good is unalloyed, of course. The length and complexity of the current nominating process, to which so much good can be ascribed, are nonetheless sources of real distraction to incumbent presidents who face renomination challenges and to other contenders who hold public office. To be sure, the post-1968 rules cannot be blamed for all of this. Unpopular presidents have always had to battle, to some extent, for renomination; popular presidents still do not. (In 1984 Reagan not only was unopposed for his party's nomination—the first such president since 1956—but received millions of dollars in federal matching funds for his renomination "campaign.") Most challengers seem to be able to arrange time to campaign, either while holding office (Gary Hart, Alan Cranston, Ernest Hollings, and others in 1984) or by abandoning office for the sake of pursuing the presidency (Walter Mondale in 1984, Howard Baker in 1988). Still, by any standard, the same nominating process that tests a would-be president's leadership skills so well must be said to carry at least a moderate price tag. . . .

Keep the Current System

There are good reasons to stay with the current arrangement. First, the very constancy of rules rewriting is in itself subversive of legitimacy. Second, it also is distracting to the parties, diverting them from the more important task of deciding what they have to offer voters. Finally, to bring the argument of this essay full circle, to the extent that the current process helps the political parties to grow stronger and the presidency to work more effectively, voters ultimately will grow not just used to it but pleased with it, and the legitimacy problem will take care of itself.

"No one has been able to show how the preservation of a quaint eighteenth-century voting device, the electoral college, . . . can serve to protect the Republic."

The Electoral College Should Be Abolished

Neal R. Peirce and Lawrence D. Longley

Many voters believe that when they vote for the president they vote for a candidate. Actually, they are voting for a slate of delegates who will represent their state in the electoral college, which officially elects the president. In the following viewpoint, Neal R. Peirce and Lawrence D. Longley claim that the electoral college could potentially bring a candidate to office who did not get the most votes. They argue in favor of abolishing the electoral college and pronouncing the candidate with the most votes nationwide to be the president. Peirce is a syndicated columnist and a contributing editor to the *National Journal*. Longley is a government professor at Lawrence University in Wisconsin.

As you read, consider the following questions:

1. What are the advantages of having direct election of presidents, according to Peirce and Longley?
2. Why do the authors think that the electoral college is not a force for moderation in American politics?
3. In what ways, according to the authors, could the electoral college put a president into office who hadn't been chosen by the majority of voters?

Neal R. Peirce and Lawrence D. Longley, *The People's President*. New Haven, CT: Yale University Press, 1981. Copyright © 1981 by Yale University.

Either the country will continue with the existing electoral college system or it will shift to a direct popular vote.

The advantages of a direct vote are immediately apparent. There would no longer be the chance that the candidate who won the most popular votes could be deprived of the presidency through the mathematical vagaries of the electoral college. The massive disfranchisement of the minority voters in each state would be ended once and for all, with each person's vote registered directly and equally in the decisive national count. No one's vote would be totally eclipsed or magnified to many times its rightful weight because of the chance factor of state residence. Localized corruption in a single large state would be far less likely to determine the outcome of the national election. The office of elector would disappear, so that no "electoral Benedict Arnold" could take it in his own hands to sway the outcome of an election. Splinter parties would no longer have the ability to shift the outcome in pivotal states or to capitalize on their strength in a handful of states to throw an election into the House of Representatives for decision. If the direct vote system were properly devised, there would no longer be the possibility of a contingent election in Congress where a prospective chief executive could be subjected to unconscionable pressures to "sell out" on major issues as the price of his election. . . .

Direct Election and Moderation

Behind the arguments of many thoughtful opponents of the direct vote is a concern that we would be substituting a kind of naked, unrestrained majoritarianism for a system that obliges the national parties and presidential candidates to offer moderate programs acceptable to a wide range of economic, geographic, and political interests. The electoral college, [political scientist] Carl Becker argued, is a major factor in forcing both political parties to hew close to the middle of the road, in deterring them from the adoption of "pure" ideologies and taking an uncompromising stand in favor of any single economic or class group. "This system," he wrote, "makes it impossible for any political party to win a national election, even though it has a majority of the popular votes cast, unless the votes it polls are properly distributed throughout the country; and no party has much chance of getting such a distribution if it represents exclusively the interests of any section or class. It can get the necessary strategic distribution of the popular vote only if it is willing to appeal to the interests of many sections and to the interests of all classes— agriculture and industry, capital and labor, rich and poor, progressives and conservatives—in a sufficient number of states to win a majority of the electoral votes.". . .

What then of Carl Becker's argument? Would direct election of the president undermine the forces working for appeasement, for

150

It's Time to Retire

© Liederman/Rothco.

conciliation, and for compromise in the American political system? Would rigid ideologies and inflammatory class appeals become more dominant? Again, there is no palpable evidence to support the allegation. In fact, it must be acknowledged that the existing system does not invariably create perfect moderation and balance in our presidential campaigns. One may admire Harry Truman's political courage in 1948, but by any dispassionate analysis it must be conceded that his campaign was based on blatant class and ethnic appeals. For uncompromising ideology, no presidential candidates of modern times have outdone Barry Goldwater in the 1964 campaign and George McGovern in the 1972 contest. These campaigns may be more the exception than the rule, but they have happened, the electoral college notwithstanding.

Every Vote Would Count

Secondly, it may be asked if the actual operation of the electoral college has anything to do with the moderation of political life in the United States. If most Americans think they are voting for president directly anyway, it is hard to see how a constitutional legitimization of their direct participation would change their attitude or that of the political leaders. It is suggested that the electoral college makes presidential candidates and parties appeal to all sections and all classes. Senator Hugh Scott of Pennsylvania, chairman of the Republican National Committee in the 1948 campaign and a strategist in the Eisenhower and Nixon races, suggested in an interview with one of this . . . [viewpoint's] authors, that the necessity of seeking state-by-state victories obliges a presidential candidate to recognize particular state and regional problems—irrigation and grazing problems in the West, the out-migration of industry in the East, TVA policies in the Tennessee Valley, or East-West trade in the Dakotas. Scott's argument—echoed by many opponents of the direct vote before and after him (we will spare the reader the dozens of possible citations)—is an interesting one; if valid it would be a compelling reason to resist the direct vote. But is it valid? Just because *states qua* states would not participate in the choice of a president, would a candidate be able to ignore vast classes or regions and have any prospect of winning? We think not. He would still have to fashion a national majority out of votes from hundreds of geographic areas, class and economic groups, and ideological camps. No single group could give him the election. In fact, the candidate might be more willing than not to consider special local problems, since every vote in every state would count—even if the opposing party was all but sure to carry that state.

A Distorted Counting Device

In the final analysis, it must be recognized that the electoral college today—barring the catastrophe of rebel electors of an election thrown into the House—is nothing more than a counting device and a highly distorted one at that. Consciously or not, every candidate for president aims first at winning the support of a majority of the whole American people, because winning an electoral college majority without a popular vote majority is a risky undertaking. Before the 1964 election Barry Goldwater's strategists thought they might achieve an electoral college victory by combining the electoral votes of the South with those of the conservative western Mountain states and the farm-oriented

Midwest. They consciously wrote off the popular-vote-heavy states like California, New York, Pennsylvania, and New Jersey, admitting, at least implicitly, a national popular vote defeat. A similar hope for electoral college victory in the face of a popular vote loss was attributed to McGovern campaign strategists in 1972, though the seriousness with which the tactic was approached is not clear. Such strategies, bankrupt from the start, predictably end in overwhelming and deserved defeat. And if no serious presidential candidate will consciously design a strategy that admits popular vote defeat in the hope of electoral college victory, would it not be better to have a popular vote alone? Even if there were predictable regional patterns that permitted a candidate to localize his campaign to win in the electoral college while losing the popular vote, would we want to accept such a system? Should westerners or southerners or people from any region, by the way the electoral votes are distributed, be accorded some special privilege in electing the president that the rest of us are denied? Indeed, if the system *did* operate this way, there would be all the more reason to abolish it posthaste.

Electoral College Is Antidemocratic

The Electoral College is an anti-democratic and potentially dangerous anachronism within our structure of government. It provides for election of the President and vice president under a state-by-state, winner-take-all system, rather than by a popular vote of the nation as a whole. It could easily lead to a situation in which a candidate won the presidency by gaining narrow majorities in enough states to prevail in the Electoral College, but who actually received fewer popular votes than his opponent. This would deprive the victorious candidate of the mandate that is so necessary to successful leadership. . . .

The Electoral College poses a constant threat to the successful functioning of the only offices that represent all the people of the United States. We should eliminate this threat by abolishing the Electoral College and replacing it with a system of direct election of the President and vice president.

Jack Brooks, *American Legion Magazine*, August 1987.

If a direct vote really did lead to increased class antagonisms, ideologically oriented campaigns, and a lack of political moderation, we should have seen these factors at work already in the states, where every governor is chosen today by direct vote of the people. The major states especially could be said to be microcosms of the entire nation. The 1960 census showed that New York and California both had four times as many inhabitants as the entire

United States in the first census, that of 1790. Yet direct vote has not led to extremism in the states; indeed, the overwhelming majority of U.S. governors have tended to be practical problem-solvers rather than ideological zealots. Nor has the Senate become a stomping ground for extremists in the wake of the 17th amendment, which shifted the selection of senators from the state legislatures to direct vote of the people.

In fact, direct vote of the people is hardly a risky, untried governmental principle that could "blow up in our faces." It is the tried and true way of electing every nonappointive governmental official in the United States today, and for the most part it has been the common rule and practice since the birth of our nation. . . .

The Electoral College and Federalism

Those who would preserve the existing electoral college because of its ties to the federal system ought to consider the effect on American federalism if the electoral college were again to elect a candidate who lost in the popular vote. How could this be explained to the people? That the voters of certain states—any way the mathematical vagaries of the electoral college might misfire—should have more weight in the election of the president than the voters of other states, which make up a majority of the country? That for some mysterious reason connected with the federal system, the votes of people from Wyoming and New Hampshire were to be given more weight than the votes of people from New York and California—or possibly the reverse? How would these inequalities be explained in the day of "one man, one vote"?

The question is by no means abstract. In 1976, for instance, our analysis has shown that the slightest variation in the electoral vote of some northern states would have elected Gerald Ford president despite Jimmy Carter's strong popular vote lead. The scenario of a potential Ford win in electoral votes while Carter won the popular vote was easy to foresee weeks before the election because of Carter's lopsided leads in many southern states that year. But consider what would have happened if Ford had actually won the electoral vote while Carter retained his popular vote lead. Would there be any rational way to explain to southerners that their votes—because they were geographically concentrated—were of less import and weight than votes cast elsewhere in America? That some hocus-pocus in an eighteenth-century vote-counting device was more important than the popular will? This is the one totally compelling, irrefutable argument that causes defenders of the existing system to founder time and again. There can be no rational explanation for retaining the arcane counting system when one projects it forward to the day that it actually causes the system to blow up in our faces again. To preserve such a system for abstract reasons incomprehensible to all but a tiny band of federalism savants would seem to be poor service to legitimate American federalism, a system and belief of immense inherent strength and importance. . . .

"A More Perfect Union"

In one respect, the proposal for abolishing the rickety old electoral college and substituting a direct vote of the people seems to be little more than a housekeeping item on the agenda of pressing national and international problems that face the American people as they enter the closing decades of the twentieth century. Yet the importance of the presidency in American life can scarcely be underestimated, and thus the way that office is filled must be a matter of major national concern. As [former presidential candidate] Estes Kefauver commented in 1961, "Every four years the electoral college is a loaded pistol aimed at our system of government. Its continued existence is a game of Russian roulette. Once its antiquated procedures trigger a loaded cylinder, it may be too late for the needed corrections."

Abolish It Now

I am in favor of abolishing the Electoral College immediately. It must not be allowed to meet even one more time. The process leading to a constitutional amendment which would eliminate at least this error must be started immediately, even though the resulting amendment might have to be superseded later when more fundamental changes became possible. All plans which have been advanced for keeping the College, but with restraints and protections, seem inherently dangerous to me and I could accept none; as long as the College existed, clever ways would be found to manipulate it. It should be given no extension of life. It should be abolished now.

James Michener, *Presidential Lottery*, 1969.

Of course, it is possible that even if the electoral college sent the popular-vote loser to the White House, the people would find a way to live with the situation—even though the authority of the presidency and the quality of American democracy would certainly be undermined. But even if one assumes that the country *could* somehow exist with a president the people had rejected, the question still remains: What good reason is there to continue such an irrational voting system in an advanced democratic nation, where the ideal of popular choice is the most deeply ingrained of governmental principles?

Democratic elections do not always guarantee that the best man will win. Even when we have scraped the barnacles of the elec-

155

toral college from the ship of state, there is no guarantee that we or our descendants may not one day elect a charlatan or an ideologue to the presidency. For all our talk of great American presidents, we have elected some pretty grim mediocrites to that office, and we could again—although we would like to believe that the modern levels of education and political sophistication in the United States today make it far less likely. But even when one admits that the *vox populi* may err, the fact remains that through our entire national experience we have learned that there is no safer, no better way to elect our public officials than by the choice of the people, with the man who wins the most votes being awarded the office. This is the essence of "the consent of the governed." And no matter how wisely or foolishly the American people choose their president, he *is* their president. No one has been able to show how the preservation of a quaint eighteenth-century voting device, the electoral college, with all its anomalies and potential wild cards, can serve to protect the Republic. The choice of the chief executive must be the people's, and it should rest with none other than them.

"There is no serious reason to quarrel with the major features of [the electoral college]."

The Electoral College Should Be Maintained

Nelson W. Polsby and Aaron Wildavsky

In the following viewpoint, Nelson W. Polsby and Aaron Wildavsky argue that the electoral college helps insure stability in government by naming a clear winner of the presidential race. They contend that without the electoral college to name a clear winner, the front runner in a close election would have to make concessions to splinter-group fractions in order to gain a sufficient number to votes. Although the authors acknowledge some problems with the electoral college, they conclude that no better system for electing presidents has been proposed. Both Polsby and Wildavsky are political science professors at the University of California, Berkeley.

As you read, consider the following questions:

1. Why do Polsby and Wildavsky believe abolishing the electoral college would give medium-sized one-party states an advantage in presidential elections?
2. According to the authors, what could be the consequences of a close presidential election held without an electoral college?
3. Why do the authors think that the dangers of a second place candidate winning the presidency through the electoral college are exaggerated?

Nelson Polsby and Aaron Wildavsky, excerpted from *Presidential Elections*, sixth edition. Copyright © 1984 Emily Polsby and the Wildavsky Children's Trusts. Reprinted with the permission of Charles Scribner's Sons, an imprint of Macmillan Publishing Company.

157

Close presidential elections, those in which the new president has only a narrow margin in the total popular vote, always lead to renewed public discussion of the merits of the Electoral College, since close elections remind people of the mathematical possibility that the candidate with a plurality of all the votes will not necessarily become president. Reform interest surges even higher when a regionally based third party, such as the party George Wallace led in 1968, becomes strong enough conceivably to prevent any candidate from having an electoral vote majority. This would drive the decision into the U.S. House of Representatives, which under the Constitution decides such matters when the Electoral College cannot. . . .

Minority Favored Under Direct Elections

Allowing a majority (or plurality) of voters to choose a president has a great deal to commend it. This is the simplest method of all; it would be most easily understood by the greatest number of people; it is the plan favored by the majority of Americans; and it comes closest to reflecting intuitive notions of direct popular sovereignty through majority rule. But to end the matter there would be too simpleminded. There is more than one political lesson to be learned by a closer examination of the Electoral College and available alternatives to it.

The outright abolition of the Electoral College, and the substitution of the direct election of the president, would certainly reduce the importance of the larger states. It would mean that the popular vote margin that a state could provide, not the number of electoral votes, would determine its importance. For example, under the present system a candidate who carries California by 144,100 votes (as Reagan did in 1980) has garnered one-sixth of the support he needs to win, while under the direct-vote system states like Massachusetts or Alabama can sometimes generate three and four times that much margin. In the two-party states, in which category most of the larger states fall, voters are cross-pressured in many ways, and a candidate can seldom count on defeating his opponent by a very large margin. The reason, then, that the large states lose influence is that this system switches influence from the close states to one-party states; in some states where one party's organization is weak, large majorities for the other party are easier to turn out at election time, and special rewards would be forthcoming for party leaders who could provide a large margin of victory for their candidate. As candidates currently look with favor on those who can bring them support in the large states, because this spells victory, so might they be expected to look with favor on those who can bring them large popular margins in the one-party states, should that become the criterion. The emphasis would not be on which candidate was going to win the state, already a foregone conclusion, but by how many votes he was going to win. The small states do not gain, however, because even when they are one-party, they are not large enough to generate substantial voting margins. Direct election thus changes the advantage from the biggest and the smallest two-party states to the medium-sized one-party states, and these, in the United States, happen most commonly to be located in the South. . . .

How one feels about this situation depends on (1) how one still feels about the diminution of large-state influence and the gain by sundry other smaller states, (2) how much of a plurality one feels a newly elected president should have, and (3) how this plurality limit will affect others in the system.

Prevents Regional Presidents

The Electoral College prevents [the] unseemly anomaly of a regional president. Because the states are the focus of the electoral process, a presidential candidate is far less likely to become the captive of a single populous state or region. . . .

The framers of the Constitution wisely built into our Constitution principles of federalism, separated powers and geographical balance to prevent rule by tyrannical majorities and powerful regional concentrations. The Electoral College has worked marvelously as a key feature of the Constitution's protective umbrella.

Orrin Hatch, *American Legion Magazine*, August 1987.

Clearly, third-party votes under a direct-election system are wasted if the candidate with a plurality wins, no matter how small that plurality; if this is how the system is made to work, it is quite possible that future "Dixiecrat"-type movements will disappear or will merge into Southern Republicanism. At best, voters could express only their anger by voting for third-party candidates and this would be at the cost of foregoing the chance to decide an election. We suspect, however, that most Americans would feel uncomfortable with a president who, even though he won a plurality, was elected by, say, only 35 percent of the voters. One of the virtues of the present electoral vote system is that it magnifies the margin of a presidential victory (as, for instance, in 1980, Reagan's 10 percent victory margin gave him 91 percent of the electoral vote), presumably conferring added legitimacy and with it acceptance of the new president's responsibility to govern in fact as well as in title. Any system of direct election would almost have to eliminate the majority principle in favor of some plurality, or it would clearly lead to much more, not less, deadlock; in three out of our past eight presidential elections, the winning candidate was without an absolute majority.

Reformers have generally agreed, though, that the winner must win by at least a substantial plurality; consequently the Electoral College reform amendment that passed the House in late 1969 provided for a runoff between the top two candidates if no one secured as much as 40 percent of the popular vote in the initial election. The first effect of this provision would be to hand back influence to third parties; if one's candidate is going to have a second chance to win the office anyway, there is an incentive for any sizable organized minority to contest the first election on its own. That the runoff would likely be used if it were provided is suggested by the 1968 figures, when there was a fairly strong third-party candidate in the race. A fourth candidate, perhaps a peace advocate, would have needed to pull only 6 or 7 percent of the national total to keep either candidate from having the required 40 percent (Nixon won with only 43.4 percent, although he had 56.2 percent of the electoral vote); a large enough minority was sufficiently concerned about this one issue to make this a real possibility. Once this becomes even a plausible expectation, there is no reason for other intense minorities not to do likewise and visions of a segregationist party, a black party, a labor party, a peace party, an ecology party, even a right-to-life party, a farmers' party, and so on, appear. Whereas one of the strong points of the present system is that it enforces a compromise by penalizing all minorities that will not come to terms, the direct-election system could well encourage a Continental European model, in which numerous groups contest the first election and then recombine for the second; at the very least, severe changes would be worked on the present convention system. Should such a result have occurred in 1968, or should it occur in the future, the simplicity, ease of comprehension, and inherent majoritarian rightness of the direct-election solution would quickly disappear. . . .

Splinter Group Victory Is Unlikely

Under the present Electoral College system, there has been no time since 1876 when any splinter group has been able to make good its threat to throw the election into the House, and in fact this is quite unlikely to occur since it requires all of the Deep South (Louisiana, Arkansas, Mississippi, Alabama, Georgia, South Carolina, North Carolina) to vote for a third party, plus a very even division in nonsouthern votes. Even in 1948 Harry Truman won an Electoral College majority despite threats from both a third and a fourth party. In spite of the mathematical possibilities, not once in this century has the loser of the popular vote become president. On the other hand a direct-election plan that required a 40 percent plurality might well have forced a runoff in 1968 and 1976. . . .

We have argued that there is no serious reason to quarrel with the major features of the present system, since in our form of government "majority rule" does not operate in a vacuum but within a system of "checks and balances.". . .

Majority rule should be placed in proper perspective by considering other aspects of democratic government, such as the principle of political equality or the need for effective government. It would not help majorities, for instance, to so fractionalize the electoral or popular vote that all presidents would be rendered ineffective. Overrepresentation of rural interests in Congress has in the past inhibited political equality. To check this inequality we either had to alter the circumstances that promoted it or provide some other means of preventing rural interests from dominating the political system. Now that the method of determining the composition of Congress has undergone change, owing to fair reapportionment, we can consider abolishing the Electoral College and turn to majority (or plurality) voting in electing presidents. Other things being equal, a simpler and more direct method would be preferable to a device as complex in operation and as difficult to understand as the Electoral College. But the probable defects and equivalent complexities of alternatives to the Electoral College thus far proposed make us skeptical that the day has yet arrived when we can say that other things are in fact equal.

Ranking Concerns in Choosing a President

Every four years the US goes through a lengthy process of choosing a president. The voters in this election bring a complex web of concerns and loyalties with them. A voting decision is often based upon striking a balance between competing concerns. For example, a voter may have to weigh loyalty to a particular party against concern for an industry in his or her region that would be affected by the election of a particular candidate. This exercise will give you the opportunity to prioritize the values you consider important when choosing a presidential candidate.

Imagine you are a voter in an upcoming primary election which has several candidates from different parties. The following table lists some of the concerns you the voter might consider in choosing a candidate. Examine this list and rank the concerns in order of importance to you in making a voting decision.

_____ candidate's opinion on a particular issue

_____ candidate's personal or family life

_____ candidate's party affiliation

_____ candidate's home state or region

_____ candidate's ability in public debates

_____ candidate's appearance, television presence

_____ candidate's previous government experience

_____ candidate's trustworthiness, honesty

_____ candidate's voting record

_____ candidate's racial or ethnic background

_____ candidate's gender

_____ endorsements candidate has received

After you have finished putting the concerns in order, answer the following questions. Then, form small groups and discuss your choices. Put together a group ranking and present it to the class. Be prepared to defend your choices.

1. What concern was the most important to you? What was the least? Explain why.

2. Is there any one concern that overrides all the others? If a candidate matched your preferences in all but one concern, which one of the listed concerns, if any, would be important enough to keep you from voting for that candidate?

3. Are there any concerns in the list that are of no importance to you? Why? Why might other people find them important?

Periodical Bibliography

The following articles have been selected to supplement the diverse views presented in this chapter.

Gloria Borger	"Campaign '88: Why Iowa Is Bad for American Politics," *U.S. News & World Report,* July 6, 1987.
Bruce Buchanan	"Open All Candidates Before Election," *The New York Times,* October 2, 1987.
Mickey Kaus	"Far Too Much Ado About Little Iowa," *Newsweek,* July 6, 1987.
Everett Carll Ladd	"Political Grumbling—and Making Do: Would We Really Want Campaigns Shorter, Less Burdensome?" *The Christian Science Monitor,* September 15, 1987.
Douglas MacArthur II	"The Choosing of the US President," *The Christian Science Monitor,* August 11, 1987.
Bob McBarton	"A Caveat for Candidates," *Newsweek,* October 19, 1987.
Austin Ranney	"Farewell to Reform—Almost," *Society,* May/June 1987.
James Reston	"The Media and the Election," *The New York Times,* March 15, 1987.
Vermont Royster	"Are You Dreaming of the White House?" *The Wall Street Journal,* April 10, 1987.
William Schneider	"The Democrats in '88," *The Atlantic Monthly,* April 1987.
William Schneider	"The Republicans in '88," *The Atlantic Monthly,* July 1987.
Paul Taylor	"Is This Any Way To Pick a President?" *The Washington Post National Weekly Edition,* April 13, 1987.
Paul Taylor	"Our People-Magazined Race for the Presidency," *The Washington Post National Weekly Edition,* November 2, 1987.

Appendix of US Political Parties

The following is a list of some of the political parties that enter candidates in national elections.

Communist Party of the United States of America (CPUSA)
235 W. 23rd St.
New York, NY 10011
(212) 989-4994

Founded in 1919, the CPUSA is dedicated to advancing the interests of "all working people and all specially oppressed peoples." It seeks to abolish the capitalist system and replace it with a socialist democracy based on state ownership and operation of industry, within a state led by the working class.

Democratic Party
Democratic National Committee
430 South Capitol St. SE
Washington, DC 20003
(202) 863-8000

The Democratic party was founded in 1798 by Thomas Jefferson as the "party of the common man." Among its many stands on the issues, the party calls for more cooperation between government to industry and improve economic growth and for more government support of education and childcare programs.

National Hamiltonian Party
3314 Dillon Road
Flushing, MI 48433
(313) 659-7384

Founded in 1965, the party seeks "to bring nobility, ability and dignity back to American government." It is named for Alexander Hamilton, first secretary of the treasury, who advocated government by an educated elite. The party is in favor of limiting the right to vote to only the most educated and prominent citizens. It has received thousands of write-in votes for its candidates in over a dozen states since its founding.

National Prohibition Party
PO Box 2635
Denver, CO 80201
(303) 572-0646

The National Prohibition party, founded in 1869, seeks the repeal of all laws that legalize the sale and use of liquor. The party also advocates a balanced budget, limits on Congress's taxation powers, a Human Life Amendment, free-market economics, and enforcement and strengthening of laws against gambling, pornography and other immoral behavior.

Libertarian Party
301 W. 21st St.
Houston, TX 77008
(713) 880-1776

Founded in 1971, the Libertarian party is the nation's third largest political party. The party advocates that each individual has the absolute right to exercise sole dominion over his or her own life, liberty and property so long as he or she also respects the rights of others. The party opposes censorship, the draft, and government regulation, and supports free trade, property rights, and an eventual end to taxation.

Peace and Freedom Party
3309 Mission St., Suite 135
San Francisco, CA 94110
(415) 387-7012

The Peace and Freedom party is a socialist electoral coalition in California. With over 40,000 registered members, it is the largest left-wing electoral party in the country. The party seeks to eliminate defense spending, reduce the work week, nationalize basic industries, centralize economic planning, abolish individual taxes, and end legal and social discrimination against women and minorities.

Republican Party
Republican National Committee
310 First St. SE
Washington, DC 20003
(202) 863-8614

The Republican party was founded in 1856. Four years later it elected its first president, Abraham Lincoln. Among its many stands on the issues, the party advocates less government regulation of the economy, lower taxes, and a continued strengthening of American military forces.

Socialist Party USA
516 W. 25th St., Suite 404
New York, NY 10001
(212) 691-0776

Founded in 1901, the Socialist party strives to establish a classless, nonracist, feminist, socialist society. It advocates government-financed healthcare, unilateral nuclear disarmament, and industries governed by workers through elections.

Organizations To Contact

The editors have compiled the following list of organizations which are concerned with the issues debated in this book. All of them have publications available for interested readers. The descriptions are derived from materials provided by the organizations themselves.

American Civil Liberties Union (ACLU)
132 W. 43rd St.
New York, NY 10036
(212) 944-9800

The ACLU champions the rights set forth in the Declaration of Independence and the Constitution. Their chapters offer legal support for plaintiffs in voting discrimination cases. Its many publications include the pamphlet *The Voting Rights Act: What It Means, How To Make It Work for You.*

American Enterprise Institute for Public Policy Research (AEI)
1150 17th St. NW
Washington, DC 20036
(202) 862-5800

AEI has published numerous books and pamphlets on topics such as presidential primaries, campaign finance, political parties, and the electoral college. Among them are *The Electoral College and the American Idea of Democracy* and *Before Nomination: Our Primary Problems.* After every national election, the Institute publishes studies on the results.

Cato Institute
224 Second St. SE
Washington, DC 20003
(202) 546-0200

In accord with the Cato Institute's belief that government should be limited and individual liberty respected, it opposes federal regulation of election campaigns. It has published a number of books on America's elections, including *Beyond Liberal and Conservative* and *Left, Right and Babyboom.* It also publishes *Policy Analyses,* a series of position papers covering such topics as campaign finance and political action committees.

Churches' Committee for Voter Registration/Education
110 Maryland Ave. NE
Washington, DC 20002
(202) 543-2800

The Churches' Committee is an ecumenical voter participation project formed in 1983. It works to increase the participation of the poor and minorities in the electoral process. The committee publishes two how-to manuals on voter registration campaigns, *Voter Education: The Missing Link* and *Voter Registration, Education, and Get Out the Vote.*

Common Cause
2030 M St. NW
Washington, DC 20036
(202) 833-1200

Common Cause, founded in 1970, is a nonprofit, nonpartisan public interest organization of more than 250,000 members. It seeks reforms in government ethics, campaign financing, and political action committees. Common Cause publishes on-going campaign finance studies, which tabulate and analyze candidate finance reports filed with the Federal Elections Commission. It also publishes articles relating to campaign finance in the bimonthly *Common Cause Magazine* and in press releases entitled *Common Cause News.*

The League of Women Voters Education Fund
1730 M St. NW
Washington, DC 20036
(202) 429-1965

The Fund is the educational arm of the League of Women Voters of the United States. The League is a voluntary organization of women and men who promote political responsibility through informed and active citizen participation in government. Since 1976, the League has sponsored debates between presidential candidates at both the primary and national levels. The Fund publishes several pamphlets, including *The Women's Vote, How To Judge a Candidate,* and *How To Watch a Debate.*

Public Affairs Council
1255 23rd St. NW, Suite 750
Washington, DC 20037
(202) 872-1790

The Public Affairs Council is a professional association of executives from corporations and other organizations. Founded in 1954, the Council publishes newsletters and reports on campaign finance and political action committees, including *The Case for PACs* and *Soft Money and Campaign Financing.*

Southwest Voter Registration Education Project (SVREP)
201 N. St. Mary's St., Suite 501
San Antonio, TX 78205
(512) 222-0224

SVREP is a nonprofit, nonpartisan organization dedicated to increasing Hispanic participation in the democratic process. It produces articles and reports on minority voting, redistricting, reapportionment, and voting rights litigation and legislation. Its monthly newsletters include *Southwest Political Report* and *Southwest Voter Research Notes.* It also publishes *The Hispanic Electorates,* a survey of Hispanic-American voting habits and political beliefs.

U.S. English
1424 16th St. NW
Washington, DC 20036
(202) 232-5200

U.S. English is a national organization founded to secure legal protection for English as the official language of the United States and to maintain the primacy of English in American public life. U.S. English publishes a discussion series and a series of fact sheets on issues of language and public policy, including bilingual ballots.

Bibliography of Books

Herbert Alexander
Financing Politics. Washington, DC: Congressional Quarterly Press, 1984.

The American Assembly, Columbia University
The Future of American Political Parties: The Challenge of Governance. Englewood Cliffs, NJ: Prentice-Hall, Inc., 1982.

Judith Best
The Case Against Direct Election of the President. Ithaca, NY: Cornell University Press, 1975.

David Boaz, ed.
Left, Right & Babyboom: America's New Politics. Washington, DC: Cato Institute, 1986.

James MacGregor Burns
The Power To Lead. New York: Simon & Schuster, 1984.

Russell J. Dalton, Scott C. Flanagan, and Paul Allen Beck, eds.
Electoral Change in Advanced Industrial Democracies. Princeton, NJ: Princeton University Press, 1984.

Robert E. DiClerico and Eric M. Uslaner
Few Are Chosen: Problems in Presidential Selection. New York: McGraw-Hill Book Company, 1984.

G. William Domhoff
Who Rules America Now? New York: Simon & Schuster, 1983.

Margaret Edds
Free at Last. Bethesda, MD: Adler & Adler Publishers, Inc., 1987.

Leon D. Epstein
Political Parties in the American Mold. Madison: The University of Wisconsin Press, 1986.

Jack W. Germond and Jules Witcover
Wake Us When It's Over: Presidential Politics of 1984. New York: Macmillan Publishing Company, 1985.

Doris Graber
Mass Media and American Politics. Washington, DC: Congressional Quarterly, 1984.

Robert Hirschfield, ed.
Selection Election: A Forum on the American Presidency. New York: Aldine Publishing Company, 1982.

Lynda Lee Kaid, Dan Nimmo, and Keith R. Sanders, eds.
New Perspectives on Political Advertising. Carbondale, IL: Southern Illinois University Press, 1986.

Gladys Engel Lang and Kurt Lang
Politics and Television Re-Viewed. Beverly Hills, CA: Sage Publications, 1984.

Richard L. McCormick, ed.
Political Parties and the Modern State. New Brunswick, NJ: Rutgers University Press, 1984.

Michael Malbin, ed.
Money and Politics in the United States. Chatham, NJ: Chatham House Publishers, 1984.

Michael Nelson, ed.
The Presidency and the Political System. Washington, DC: Congressional Quarterly Press, 1984.

W. Russell Neuman
The Paradox of Mass Politics. Cambridge, MA: Harvard University Press, 1986.

Michael Parenti
Democracy for the Few. New York: St. Martin's Press, 1983.

Nelson W. Polsby
Consequences of Party Reform. New York: Oxford University Press, 1983.

169

Austin Ranney

Channels of Power. New York: Basic Books, 1983.

A. James Reichley, ed.

Elections American Style. Washington, DC: The Brookings Institution, 1987.

Steven L. Rosenstone, Roy L. Behr, and Edward H. Lazarus

Third Parties in America. Princeton, NJ: Princeton University Press, 1984.

Stephen A. Salmore and Barbara G. Salmore

Candidates, Parties, and Campaigns. Washington, DC: Congressional Quarterly Books, 1985.

Kay L. Schlozman, ed.

Elections in America. Winchester, MA: Allen & Unwin, 1987.

Burton D. Sheppard

Rethinking Congressional Reform. Cambridge, MA: Schenkman Books, 1985.

Theodore C. Sorensen

A Different Kind of Presidency. New York: Harper & Row, 1984.

Abigail M. Thernstrom

Whose Votes Count? Cambridge, MA: Harvard University Press, 1987.

Index

Alexander, Herbert, 72
American Civil Liberties Union, 31
Avakian, Bob, 22

Baker, Ross K., 111
Baker v. *Carr,* 28
Barnes, Fred, 123
Bates, Stephen, 121
Beckel, Robert G., 115
Becker, Carl, 150
bilingual ballots
  are hardly used, 40
  are often used, 46, 48
  costs of, 40, 41
  in the Southwest, 46-47
  should be used, 45-48
  should not be used, 39-44
bilingualism
  causes segregation, 41-43
Block, Herb, 81
Blume, Keith, 94
Bolling, Richard, 56, 79
Brischetto, Robert R., 45
Broder, David S., 100, 109, 144
Brooks, Jack, 153
Buckley v. *Valeo,* 79
Byrd, Robert, 58

campaign advertising, 106
  and TV spots
    are informative, 99, 106, 123
    are not informative, 118-120
  can increase voting, 122
  is harmful, 117-120
  is not harmful, 121-124
  money spent on, 119-120, 122
campaign financing
  amounts spent, 60, 61, 68-69, 75,
    80
  and First Amendment, 60-62, 71,
    73, 80
  and full disclosure, 55, 73, 76
  and incumbents, 83, 84, 86, 87
  and independent expenditures, 80
  and political parties, 82-83, 86-88
  and presidential elections, 55
  and Supreme Court, 79-80, 87-88
  corrupts politics, 55-58, 60
    con, 60-62
  distorts democratic process, 57-58
  limits on, 55
  reform of
    is necessary, 54-58, 78
    is unnecessary, 59-62, 86
  should include government funds,

    77-84
    con, 85-88
candidates
  do not have a right to privacy,
    108-110
  have a right to privacy, 111-116
Carter, Jimmy, 95, 102, 103, 104,
  113, 140, 154
Castro, Richard T., 47
Commission on Party Structure and
  Delegate Selection, 138, 142
Common Cause, 60, 61, 64, 68, 75,
  83
Conrad, Paul, 119
Cooper, Matthew, 36
Cronin, Thomas E., 134

Diamond, Edwin, 121
DiClerico, Robert E., 21
Drew, Elizabeth, 54, 83
Durenburger, David, 74

Edwards, Don, 37
Eisenhower, Dwight D., 112, 137,
  138
elections
  and media, *see* media
  are controlled by ruling class,
    23-25
  focus on personalities, 103-104
electoral college
  should be abolished, 149-156, 158
  should be maintained, 150, 157-161

Fahrenkopf, Frank J., 85
Federal Election Campaign Act, 87-88
Ford, Gerald, 40, 104, 154
Frickey, Philip P., 27

Gamble, Ed, 19, 65
Germond, Jack, 104
gerrymandering, 37-38
Goldwater, Barry, 152, 153

Hart, Gary, 64, 108, 110, 112-114,
  148
Hatch, Orrin, 159
Hayakawa, S.I., 43, 44
Holt, Pat M., 117
Hoover, J. Edgar, 112
Humphrey, Hubert, 131

Inouye, Daniel, 55

Johnson, Lyndon, 103, 112, 137

Keefe, Mike, 113
Kefauver, Estes, 139, 155
Kennedy, John F., 112, 131, 134, 138
Kerry, John, 69
King, Martin Luther, 28, 112, 114
Kinsley, Michael, 107
Kirkpatrick, Jeane, 145
Kolb, Richard K., 39
Koppel, Ted, 95

Ladd, Everett Carll, 145, 147
LaRouche, Lyndon, 19, 87
Leadership Conference on Civil
  Rights, 36, 37
Locher, Dick, 24
Loevy, Robert D., 134
Longley, Lawrence D., 149

McCarthy, Eugene, 74-75, 86, 131
McGovern, George, 137-139, 152, 153
Malbin, Michael, 60, 87
Manatt, Charles T., 130
Mathias, Charles McC., 67, 77
media
  and campaigns, 24, 25, 72, 73
    have a negative influence, 95-99
    how to improve, 105-106
    should focus on issues, 94-99
    should focus on who is winning,
      100-106
  and candidates' private lives
    should not report on, 11-116
    should report on, 108-110
Mexican American Legal Defense
  and Educational Fund (MALDEF),
  46
Michener, James, 155
Mondale, Walter, 23, 96-98, 148

National Association of Latin
  Elected and Appointed Officials, 47
National Conservative Political
  Action Committee (NCPAC), 80, 88
National Council of La Raza, 40
Nelson, Michael, 141
Nixon, Richard, 55, 122, 131

O'Connell, Mary, 17

Patterson, Thomas, 102
Peirce, Neal R., 149
Pfaff, William, 139
political action committees (PACs)
  allow citizen participation, 66,
    72-76
  amounts contributed, 65-67
  are beneficial, 61, 70-76
  are detrimental, 56

are too powerful, 63-69, 79
  corrupt politics, 64-69
  definition of, 63, 71
Polsby, Nelson W., 157
presidential candidates
  skills needed, 146-148
presidential elections
  and party system, 158-159
    history of reforms, 142-146, 160
    should be stronger, 136-140
  and primary system
    convention problems, 136-137
    history of, 137-139, 142
    is effective, 141-148
    reform suggestions, 133-134, 139,
      140
    should be reformed, 130-134
    should be weakened, 135-140
  by electoral college, 157-161
  by popular vote, 149-156, 158

Rather, Dan, 96
Reagan, Ronald, 23, 96-98, 102-105
Robinson, Donald L., 135
Roosevelt, Franklin, 98, 103, 109,
  112, 114

Safire, William, 111
Samuelson, Robert J., 59
Schlafly, Phyllis, 70
Schmertz, Herb, 98
Schuck, Peter H., 32
Sorauf, Frank, 61, 66
Southwest Voter Registration
  Education Project, 46-47
Stevenson, Adlai, 138, 139
Stone, W. Clement, 55

Thernstrom, Abigail, 33-35, 37-38, 40
Thurmond, Strom, 33, 34-35
Trever, John, 132
Truman, Harry, 151

U.S. English, 41, 43, 44
Uslaner, Eric M., 21

voter turnout
  is declining, 120, 122
voting
  and apathy, 18-21, 28, 139-140
  and capitalism, 25-26
  and civil rights, 28-31
  and electoral college
    should be abolished, 149-156, 158
    should be maintained, 157-161
  and immigrants, 28, 40, 41
  as useless, 22-26, 28
  is controlled by mass media, 24, 25

promotes democracy, 17-21
reasons against, 19-20
reasons for, 18-19, 21
registration for, 18, 20
will not change society, 22-26,
  30-31
Voting Rights Act
  and bilingual ballots, 39-40, 46, 47
  harms minorities, 32-38
  helps minorities, 27-31
Voting Rights Act Amendments of
  1982, 29

Wallace, George, 33
Walters, Robert, 67
Watergate, 55, 57, 73, 104, 112, 132
Wertheimer, Fred, 60-63, 83
White, Theodore, 95
Wicker, Tom, 117
Wildavsky, Aaron, 157
Witcover, Jules, 104
Wright, Don, 137

Yzaguirre, Raul, 40